Walking with Jesus
through the Old Testament

Walking with Jesus through the Old Testament

Devotions for Lent

Paul Stroble

WESTMINSTER
JOHN KNOX PRESS
LOUISVILLE • KENTUCKY

First edition
Published by Westminster John Knox Press
Louisville, Kentucky

15 16 17 18 19 20 21 22 23 24—10 9 8 7 6 5 4 3 2 1

Book design by Sharon Adams
Cover design by Barbara LeVan Fisher / levanfisherstudio.com and Allison Taylor

Library of Congress Cataloging-in-Publication Data
Stroble, Paul E., 1957-
 Walking with Jesus through the Old Testament : devotions for Lent / Paul Stroble.
  pages cm
 ISBN 978-0-664-26121-4 (alk. paper)
 1. Lent--Prayers and devotions. 2. Bible--Devotional use. I. Title.
 BV85.S7465 2015
 242'.34--dc23

                                                    2015026177

♾ The paper used in this publication meets the minimum requirements of the American National Standard for Information Sciences—Permanence of Paper for Printed Library Materials, ANSI Z39.48-1992.

Most Westminster John Knox Press books are available at special quantity discounts when purchased in bulk by corporations, organizations, and special-interest groups. For more information, please e-mail SpecialSales@wjkbooks.com.

Contents

Introduction   vii

Week 1: Beginnings   1
Week 2: Jesus' Early Years   15
Week 3: Jesus' Ministry   35
Week 4: Jesus and Our Well-Being   55
Week 5: Great Themes of Salvation   75
Week 6: Jesus and Other Biblical Figures   95
Holy Week   113

Notes   139

Introduction

"Then [Jesus] said to them, 'Oh, how foolish you are, and how slow of heart to believe all that the prophets have declared! Was it not necessary that the Messiah should suffer these things and then enter into his glory?' Then beginning with Moses and all the prophets, he interpreted to them the things about himself in all the scriptures" (Luke 24:25–27).

This passage has always intrigued me. It's from the story of the walk to Emmaus (Luke 24:13–49), where the unrecognized, risen Christ appears to two friends, Cleopas and his unnamed companion. They recount to him their disappointment and grief concerning the fate of Jesus, and their confusion about reports of his missing body. Jesus responds with the words of this passage. Once they arrive at Emmaus, the friends invite him to stay. Finally they recognize him as he breaks the bread, but he vanishes. "Were not our hearts burning within us," they remark, "while he was opening the scriptures to us?" They ran all the way back to Jerusalem and told the disciples. Soon Jesus appeared to all of them, bid them peace, and explained to the whole group how the laws of Moses, the prophets, and the Psalms were fulfilled in Jesus' suffering, death, and resurrection.

Clearly it was important for Jesus to explain the continuity of the Scriptures with himself. But what Scriptures did Jesus open for them? That is what captures my imagination.

I love the Old Testament and love to study it. I know that many Christians do not. They want to get right to the message of Jesus contained in the New Testament, and I certainly understand that. We also gravitate right away to the Psalms, and perhaps the Proverbs and a few other books. But other sections of the Old Testament—with its ancient laws, some violent history, and seemingly disjointed content of the prophetic books—seem difficult to connect to the concerns of one's faith and everyday life. We'd rather focus on the parts that have to do more clearly with Christian experience.

The sad thing is that the Old Testament, while open to different interpretations and areas of study, is indeed filled with amazing teachings that connect richly to Christian life and experience. The foundational ideas of the Old Testament are foundational for the New Testament, too: the oneness of God, creation, covenant, the kingdom of God, atonement, redemption, the Hebrew people, holiness, ethics, and others. We can discover many areas of continuity between the two testaments. But, like Jesus' friends, we need time to deepen our understanding.

Emmaus was about seven miles from Jerusalem, and assuming a typical walking pace, Jesus might have talked for two or three hours. How wonderful if we knew what passages Jesus explained to his friends! While not presuming to know, I've built this Lenten study around the Old Testament texts that Jesus and the New Testament writers used to show how he fulfilled the Scriptures. We'll see how Jesus' experiences and teachings create links and connections among passages from different parts of the Old Testament, illustrating God's faithfulness across generations.

For each of these forty days of Lent, we'll study passages together and pray over them. We'll think about how to apply them to our lives as we devote Lenten time to the Lord. We'll learn more about Jesus, his days on earth, his death and resurrection, and all his blessings and works that he gives to us freely. We'll use the Lenten season to gain a deeper sense of Christ's presence in our lives, for the sake of spiritual growth. Let us join together and allow the Lord to teach us as we proceed toward Jerusalem and Easter!

I am solely responsible for the interpretations in this book, but I want to express appreciation for some of the "communities" of my life: Webster Hills United Methodist Church, Webster University, and Eden Theological Seminary. I also thank Sr. Annie Stevens, who provided me with the Sisters of Loretto prayer; Jessica Miller Kelley, Julie Tonini, and Alison Wingfield with Westminster John Knox Press for their tremendous help and expertise; the Webster Groves Starbucks, where I often work; and the many good friends and family members with whom I keep in touch via Facebook. My early mentor Rabbi Albert Plotkin taught me always to love and respect Christianity's Jewish heritage. I dedicate this book with love and gratitude to my family, Beth and Emily (and our cats), and also to my dear friend Stacey Stachowicz and her family.

Ash Wednesday

Ashes to Ashes

Genesis 3:15–19

My personal faith received a strange boost when I was in eighth and ninth grades and four close relatives died within a fourteen-month time period. They were members of the older generation, family members who had been influential to my life and faith.

Tragedy and distress can be impediments and even destroyers of faith, but they can be spurs to faith as well. Those successive funerals taught me at an impressionable age that we never know what's ahead in life. Within a few years, this insight became fundamental to my growing faith. I knew firsthand that we aren't necessarily protected from unexpected losses and different kinds of trouble, so if I wanted to live a faithful, meaningful life, I'd better not delay.

On Ash Wednesday, we intentionally focus upon our mortality. Several Bible verses poetically refer to us as dust and ashes. Genesis 3:19, part of our Scripture for today, reads, "you are dust, and to dust you shall return." In Genesis 18:27, Abraham refers to himself as "I who am but dust and ashes," an image also used in Job 30:19. Thus, many of us spend part of the day with black smudges of ash on our foreheads. We remind other people of their mortality too.

The Hebrew word *adam* means human being, while the word *adama* means earth. (Similarly, the English word "human" is

1

related to the Latin word *humus*, also meaning earth.) We are paradoxical: although dirt, dust, and ashes, we are made in God's image (Gen. 1:26–27) and blessed by God with many gifts and with dominion over the earth. "What a piece of work is a man," declares Shakespeare's *Hamlet*, giving us the phrase that we use to describe someone who is odd or difficult. "How noble in reason! how infinite in faculty! in form, in moving, how express and admirable! in action how like an angel! in apprehension how like a god! . . . And yet, to me, what is this quintessence of dust?"

It's good to be reminded of who we are, of our dual nature. Often we go through life making ourselves the heroes of our own stories; we subconsciously think (to paraphrase Oswald Chambers) that God can hardly function without our involvement in God's plans. Ash Wednesday is a solemn but potentially freeing time, when we're reminded of our mortality and humbleness and—ideally—let it humble our attitudes with how we approach the world and make us grow in love for God and one another, because we don't have unlimited time to show love and care for one another.

A wonderful thing about God's grace is that there is Good News within the sobering news and the soul-searching. Verse 15 is also a traditional messianic text, the earliest passage in the Bible that, according to many interpreters, points to Christ: "I will put enmity between you [the serpent] and the woman, and between your offspring and hers; he will strike your head, and you will strike his heel." The offspring is any human being, but in a messianic interpretation, the offspring referred to is Christ himself and the serpent is Satan. As John Wesley, for instance, discusses in his notes on the Bible, Christ suffers and dies as a result of his human nature—the curse of human beings to endure these things—which is Satan "bruising his heel." But Christ's sufferings are, in turn, his "striking the head" of Satan, that is, a lethal blow against Satan's power to defeat human beings with sin and death.

Here is a great promise embedded within the curse of human beings: suffering and death have no ultimate power for us, thanks to Christ. He redeems us from our sins, comforts us in our pain, and saves us to eternal life when we die.

Our Lenten journey begins on Ash Wednesday and, in some ways, our whole journey echoes the season's first day. We recognize our frailty, our wrongdoing, our mortality, and our need for grace. We know that at the end of the journey is Christ's glorious resurrection, which gives us hope and grace for all our lives.

Prayer

Dear Lord, in whose image we are created: today, help me realize that I am ashes and dust and yet richly loved and blessed by you, because Christ himself became ashes and dust on our behalf. Amen.

Digging Deeper

- Attend an Ash Wednesday service today if you are able, and write down your feelings about it. Imagine that Christ is telling you today, "I died, too, even though I wanted to live, just like you want to. But because I died and rose, your physical death is not the end for you, either!" Think about what eternal life means for you.
- In Romans 5:12–21, the apostle Paul writes about how the grace of Christ overcomes the sin introduced by Adam. Think about how that is true. Since sin is so strong in the world, why does Paul affirm that grace is stronger?

Thursday

God with Us

Isaiah 7:14–16; Matthew 1:18–25

As we move into the Lenten season, we think about the ways that we're growing and struggling in our faith. We sometimes ask God for help in the way of signs that God hears and cares. "Give me a sign!" is the way many of us have related to God at one time or another.

God has given me many "signs." Some were like Gideon's, assurances (if not so miraculous as his in Judg. 6:36–40) for my struggling faith. But I never asked for most of the signs. I recall getting a piece of distressing mail, some business matters I needed to attend to for my ailing mother. At that moment, one of my best friends called to say hello. In the early days in our marriage when money was tight, sometimes unexpected cash came in, such as a dividend check from the insurance company.

Our lesson today is a famous one for the Advent and Christmas seasons. It's a story of a divine sign that, in time, was fulfilled. In Isaiah's time, the kingdom of Judah was under threat from surrounding kingdoms. God sent Isaiah to Judah's king Ahaz, and through Isaiah, the Lord encouraged Ahaz to seek any sign he wanted. But Ahaz would not do so. His refusal, though humble sounding, indicated his struggling faith. Isaiah announced that the Lord would provide a sign anyway:

> Look, the young woman is with child and shall bear a son, and shall name him Immanuel. He shall eat curds and honey by the time he knows how to refuse the evil and choose the good. For before the child knows how to refuse the evil and choose the good, the land before whose two kings you are in dread will be deserted. (Isa. 7:14–16)

In the original context, the young woman is not identified. Nor

4

does the original Hebrew word specify whether or not she was a virgin. At this stage, the verse's main focus is that God exists and is present among his people. The young woman and her son Immanuel constituted a sign for the king, that God is doing new and amazing things for his kingdom and city (Jerusalem) that is for the time being under threat.

As time moved on, the Old Testament was translated into Greek, and the Greek word for "virgin" was used in translating the Hebrew word for "young woman," narrowing its meaning somewhat. As time moved further on, this passage was connected to Mary: a young woman who had never slept with a man, who became pregnant with Jesus by the power of God's Spirit. Isaiah's text became endowed with new and amazing meaning beyond its original context.

Remember that the young woman of Isaiah's prophecy is now, in the Lenten story, the middle aged woman who stands sorrowfully as her son slowly dies. Although we Protestants tend to recall Mary mostly at Christmastime, keep in mind that Isaiah's prophecy also connects us to the sorrowful, horrified Mary of Good Friday. She is a powerful pioneer of faith amid our own sorrows.

Imagine that Jesus selected this Isaiah passage for explanation to his friends en route to Emmaus. He would have talked about what it means for God to be with us. He might have said how God was present in him (Jesus) and how, very soon, God's Spirit would make Jesus more available than he had ever been in his time on earth. The faith of the young virgin woman and the power of her son were soon to bless people throughout the Roman Empire and, eventually, the whole world. All this came to pass after that special sign, given to a fearful king centuries ago.

Prayer

Holy Immanuel, you who are Lord of Life, your virgin mother bore you in a stable so that we might share your glory. Help me have a strong sense that you are truly with me. Have patience with my struggles and fill me with your grace. In Christ's name. Amen.

Digging Deeper
Think about "signs" from God. Have you had any? If so, what were they like? How did they bolster your faith? If you asked for a sign, did it come to pass right away, after a while, or not at all? What are other ways you gain confidence for your faith?

Friday

You, O Bethlehem

Micah 5:2; Luke 2:4–7

If we were on the Emmaus Road with Jesus, he might begin talking about how the Messiah must come from Bethlehem, the city of David. You might say, "Wait a minute. Bethlehem is near Jerusalem, but I thought Jesus came from Nazareth up north in Galilee." Then Jesus would explain that special circumstances forced Mary and Joseph to journey down to Bethlehem. He would explain how God's providence works in mysterious ways so that ancient and contemporary plans might be fulfilled.

Micah lived in the 700s BCE. There were other towns named Bethlehem, so he singled out Bethlehem of the region of Ephrathah as the significant place. It is the area of Rachel's tomb (Gen. 35:18–20), the village of Ruth (Ruth 4:11), and especially the birthplace of Ruth's great-grandson, King David.

The Israelite monarchy had a difficult time getting started. If you read the stories of Samuel, Saul, and David in 1 Samuel, you'll see that not everyone, including Samuel, thought a king was a good idea, since the Lord is Israel's true king. The first king, Saul, fared less well than his successor, David, who caught the imagination of Israel. David became the standard that no other king would meet, although his son Solomon was widely known and honored for his wisdom, wealth, and reign.

With the Babylonian destruction of Jerusalem (told at the end of 2 Kings), over four hundred years after David's time, the monarchy ended. But the hope of a king like David remained very strong. Isaiah 11:1 refers to a "shoot . . . from the stump of Jesse": like a new plant will grow from a tree stump, a new king will grow from David's family line (in this case, poetically rendered with reference to David's father). Other Scriptures, like our Micah passage, look with hope to a king in the lineage of David, who would even emerge from David's own home village!

7

I visited Bethlehem in 1983. The Church of the Nativity is a famous Bethlehem shrine. The opening of the door is fairly short, so nearly everyone who enters must bow. The original church was commissioned in the fourth century to stand on the site of the cave where, according to ancient traditions, Jesus was born. Although beneath the basilica, the place no longer looks like a cave. The marble floor beneath one altar has a fourteen-pointed star that is lit with silver lamps. Another altar in the church marks the traditional site where Mary placed Jesus in a manger.

Even if we've never visited Bethlehem, most of us probably have formed a sense of the town in our imaginations because of years of holiday carols. But the town doesn't have to remain a solely Christmas association; think about how timely this hymn verse is for any time of the year.

How silently, how silently
The wondrous gift is given!
So God imparts to human hearts
The blessings of His heaven.
No ear may hear His coming,
But in this world of sin,
Where meek souls will receive him still,
The dear Christ enters in.

Just as we look to Bethlehem during Advent and Christmas, we look there now, during Lent. That's because Jesus' "coronation" as a king in David's line took place on the cross! The cross, but also the subsequent resurrection, are the ways we know that Jesus is king. Thus Bethlehem, the birthplace of two kings, is a Lent and Easter town for us, too.

Prayer

Holy God, may the fact that you laid a foundation for Christ in centuries of ancient Scriptures be a source of confidence for my faith and a blessing to me. Bless us, and all our families, bless our friends and neighbors, and increase in us your mercy and compassion. In Jesus' name. Amen.

Digging Deeper
- List five places that are important to you. They may be associated with family, or they may be places you love because of their beauty or because you "recharge" there. If you can, visit one or more of those places as soon as you're able and spend time there praying and reflecting upon your Lenten journey.
- The Gospels include genealogies of Jesus (Matt. 1:1–17; Luke 3:23–38). Consider looking up some of Jesus' ancestors in a Bible dictionary. Think about what kinds of people comprise his family, both notable and notorious.

Saturday

A Child Is Born

Isaiah 9:1–7; Isaiah 11:1–9; Jeremiah 23:5–6

Among my childhood keepsakes is my collection of political pin-back buttons. Slogans like "I Like Ike" and "LBJ for the USA" and "Nixon's the One" remind me of the hopes that we have whenever we vote for our leaders.

Our Scriptures for today are filled with hope and promise for the future. To me, these passages are among the most beautiful in the Bible.

> For a child has been born for us,
>   a son given to us;
> authority rests upon his shoulders;
>   and he is named
> Wonderful Counselor, Mighty God,
>   Everlasting Father, Prince of Peace.
> His authority shall grow continually,
>   and there shall be endless peace . . .
>   (Isa. 9:6–7)

> A shoot shall come out from the stump of Jesse,
> and a branch shall grow out of his roots.
> The spirit of the LORD shall rest on him,
>   the spirit of wisdom and understanding,
>   the spirit of counsel and might,
>   the spirit of knowledge and the fear of the LORD.
> His delight shall be in the fear of the LORD.
>   (Isa. 11:1–3)

The days are surely coming, says the Lord, when I will raise up for David a righteous Branch, and he shall reign as king and deal wisely, and shall execute justice and righteousness in the land. (Jer. 23:5)

David is significant in several ways. He was successful militarily and politically. He captured the Jebusite city of Jerusalem, made it the center of the kingdom, and brought the Ark of the Covenant there. He was faithful to the Lord and sought divine guidance, making him a person "after God's own heart." When he realized he had failed and sinned, he admitted his sin and sought God's pardon. He was compassionate and sought opportunities for kindness. He sang praises and prayers to God, and some of these traditionally attributed to David are found in the book of Psalms. When we get to our Holy Week Scriptures, we'll see how images from David's psalms, centuries before Jesus, virtually describe Jesus' experiences of suffering.

Solomon succeeded David. After Solomon's death, the kingdom split into the northern and southern (Israel, also called Ephraim, and Judah) kingdoms. All of the northern kings did evil in God's sight. This faithlessness led to the fall of the northern kingdom in 722 BCE. Other than Hezekiah and Josiah, the several kings of both kingdoms were mediocre to very bad. The leadership of God's people let them down, to say the least.

But David remained a symbol of Israel's future hope and a foreshadowing of God's promises. Passages of post-exilic hope include beautiful passages about a righteous king who would rule the people with justice, who would bring peace and well-being.

It's human nature to have high expectations for our leaders, and often enough, we're disappointed. We know that Jesus was acclaimed on Palm Sunday and in a few days was on trial. But what are our own expectations for Jesus? Ask yourself: How is Jesus your "wonderful counselor"? How is Jesus your faithful and just monarch, your guarantee of peace (Isa. 9:6–7)? How does Jesus provide well-being to you, which you can even perceive in the world around you (Isa. 11:6–9)?

For being royalty, Jesus seems so low-key, even from his birth. My family and I have visited homes of royal families, like

Buckingham Palace in London and the Schönbrunn Palace in Vienna. God's own Son had no such luxury. There is a paradox at work here, a mystery: God is fulfilling a centuries-old hope, but in a lowly, even obscure way. Will God work in our own lives in bold, clear ways, or in quiet ways, through scarcely a hush?

Prayer

King Jesus, we struggle with leadership. We complain about the leaders we elect. We do understand the idea of a monarch, and yet the kind of monarch you are is confusing. Grant us clarity about who you are, our Ruler and Counselor. Amen.

Digging Deeper

- Are you "star struck" by monarchs? What is it about royalty that fascinates? What is it about leadership that raises our expectations?
- Have you ever felt disappointed in your faith? What happened? How did you solve the problem (or did you put it on hold for a while)? What would you tell someone else if they felt let down by God?

First Sunday Reflection

When I was a little boy, I thought it strange that we celebrated Jesus' birth at Christmas and then, just a few weeks later, we began to think about his death and resurrection. Jesus sure grew up fast.

I knew little about the liturgical calendar or the way the church commemorates different aspects of Jesus' life at different times of year. But now, I think my childhood wonder and confusion wasn't completely off target. We celebrate the whole of Jesus' life within the span of a year: from his birth through his relatively unknown younger years, to his ministry, and then his passion, death, and resurrection (not to mention his ascension and the subsequent Pentecost gift of the Holy Spirit). Everything about Jesus is important for our lives, and one part of his life connects with another part.

Another thing that I thought was strange when I was a little boy: Jesus was Jewish. I'm from a small Midwestern town and knew only a few Jewish people as a child. Now I understand that one of the beautiful things about Jesus' life and experience is his deep rootedness in the Jewish tradition and Scriptures.

This week's Scriptures have seemed awkward to study, because we normally associate them with Advent and Christmas. But this is the whole experience of Jesus. Even as we reflect on him during Lent, we meditate upon his roots in the scriptural hope for a great king like David. We think about the aspects of the future king's birth within the ancient prophecies. We even go all the way back to the beginning of Genesis, when human sin began, to see the beginning of God's mighty acts of blessing and salvation throughout the Jewish Scriptures. We not only study Jesus' life but also the way his coming was rooted in God's plans across the centuries.

Prayer

Dear Lord, I become stuck in my small plans and affairs. Then I realize that your plans are vast and deep and they span eons of history, light years of space, and bless billions of people. Help me join my little experiences, hopes, and dreams to the wonders of your grace. In Jesus' name. Amen.

Digging Deeper

What aspects of the Christmas season are things you'd rather not think about the rest of the year? (Frantic shopping may be one; Christmas carols sound strange any time besides December.) What aspects of the season are good to keep in your heart all year? Make a "Christmas list" of wonderful things about that season that can help your faith year-round, and in particular during this Lenten journey.

Monday

Slaughter of the Innocents

Hosea 11:1; Jeremiah 31:15–17; Matthew 2:13–19

L ife is unfair for all of us, but in different ways. We must not envy the good fortune of others because they may be struggling with some awful unfairness. Disappointments, illness, outcomes of bad choices (our own and others), and tragedies are inevitable to all. Sometimes God works miracles within our circumstances; sometimes God gives us strength to hang on.

On Ash Wednesday we thought about mortality. Today we run directly into the way life can turn horrible. An angel told Joseph to take Mary and Jesus to Egypt, for Herod sought the child's life. The Gospel notes, "This was to fulfill what had been spoken by the Lord through the prophet, 'Out of Egypt I have called my son'" (Matt. 2:15).

Meanwhile, a furious Herod ordered all the children under two years old in the Bethlehem area to be killed. The Gospel notes that

> Then was fulfilled what had been spoken through the prophet Jeremiah:
> "A voice was heard in Ramah,
>   wailing and loud lamentation,
> Rachel weeping for her children;
>   she refused to be consoled, because they are no more."
> (Matt. 2:17–18)

15

What do these Old Testament passages teach us? First, we should note that Jesus' story parallels one of the first times that non-Jews caused suffering among the Hebrews: when Pharaoh ordered the death of Hebrew babies because he feared the people were becoming too strong and numerous. But Moses was sent down the Nile in a basket and was retrieved by Pharaoh's daughter. Thus, both Moses and Jesus escaped death.

Those words in Matthew 2:15, "Out of Egypt I called my son," are from Hosea 11:1. Long after the days of Moses, God speaks of rescuing the people in an analogous way as God saved the Hebrew slaves from Pharaoh. God struggles with punishing the people for their sins, but in this section of Hosea, God expresses maternal love and a desire to nurture. This leads us to the second fulfilled text, from Jeremiah.

The prophet Jeremiah lived at the time of the Babylonian destruction of Jerusalem and the exile of the people into Babylon. Over a hundred years after Hosea's time, God finally does execute judgment. But the text speaks of Rachel, a Bible character from centuries earlier.

In Genesis, Rachel was Jacob's beloved wife and the mother of his youngest sons, Joseph and Benjamin. Rachel died giving birth to Benjamin (Gen. 35:16–20).

Though she did not raise her children, Jews have considered her a beloved figure of motherhood. She was the ancestor of the people of the northern kingdom via her two sons. (The northern kingdom was called Ephraim after the son of Joseph.) After the Assyrians conquered those Israelite tribes in 722 BCE, Rachel was honored as a mother who grieved her children and interceded for them. This is how our text from Jeremiah depicts her.[1]

Thus Rachel has similarities with another Jewish woman, Mary. As Rachel became an example of suffering motherhood in Judaism, Mary becomes an analogous example within Christian tradition. At the beginning of Jesus' life, she must face the fear, inconvenience, and confusion of having to relocate to a land many miles away as the family goes into Egyptian exile. At the end of his life, Mary has to face the death of her son. The two women had different events in their lives, but they are similarly beloved.

Today's story is an early indication that Jesus suffers along with his people and suffers as one of them. Why God allows terrible things to happen is a perennially difficult question. Even as a baby, Jesus is in the midst of grieving people, a sign that God takes our pain seriously, lives among us, and fills our life with tender care when we, too, mourn.

Prayer

Child of Bethlehem, God of Rachel and Mary: help us when we struggle with life's unfair things, with life's tragedies and horrors. During this season, help us to find peace and healing within our own circumstance, and show us anew how to support one another. Amen.

Digging Deeper

- Reread the Hosea passage and think about God's maternal aspects. How does God express love in ways we might associate as more feminine than masculine?
- Think about the idea of "peace on earth." It's a theme of several Christmas carols. But since the time of Jesus there have been innumerable conflicts and wars, some declared by Christians themselves. Does Jesus really bring peace on earth? If so, what kind of peace?

Tuesday

He Dwells among Us

Exodus 29:43–46; John 1:14; 2:19–21

Do you associate certain holidays with travel? My and my wife's parents are gone now, but for many years, we traveled to visit them on certain holidays, especially Christmas.

Synagogues were (and are) important worship and teaching places, but sacrifices and other ceremonies were done in the Temple, and, at different times of the year, faithful Jews traveled there for sacred festivals. Psalms 120–134 are songs associated with pilgrims traveling the roads up to Jerusalem for the festivals. Jesus surely had lifelong memories of traveling to the Temple, seeing it, experiencing the crowds, the sounds of voices and animals.

He first went there as an infant. Forty days following his birth, and after his circumcision (Luke 2:21), his parents presented him in the Temple for the purification ceremony and redemption of the firstborn son (Luke 2:22–38; see Lev. 12). The righteous Simeon and the prophet Anna paid him homage at that time (Luke 2:25–38). We also know the story of when his parents accidentally left him during an extended-family pilgrimage to the Temple (Luke 2:41–52). At the other end of his life, he drove the moneychangers from the Temple and taught there during his final week. Finally, according to the Gospels, the curtain of the Temple was ripped at the moment of Jesus' death, symbolizing new access to God (e.g., Matt. 27:51).

The Temple was an integral part of Jesus' life. *But he himself was a temple*, the dwelling place of God (John 2:19–21). John writes, "And the Word became flesh and lived [dwelled] among us, and we have seen his glory, the glory as of a father's only son, full of grace and truth" (John 1:14).

Here is how writers like John understood that fulfillment. In the early days, the tabernacle was a tent that the Israelites carried with them through the wilderness.[2] Accompanying the tent was the ark of the covenant, a portable box of acacia wood covered with gold that contained the tablets of the law. The cover of the ark was called the mercy seat, and the sacrificial blood sprinkled on it "covered" people's sins (Lev. 16:14–15). When the tabernacle was set up, it was the place where God's special presence dwelled, in the holiest inner room where the ark was placed, concealed by a curtain (Ex. 26:31–35).

Later, the first Temple in Jerusalem replaced the tabernacle. Solomon supervised construction of the Temple, and the ark of the covenant was located in the innermost part of the Temple called the Holy of Holies. There, God's glory had a new dwelling place but was still among God's people.

But as God became more displeased with the people, God's judgment loomed. Ezekiel 10 describes the departure of God's glory from Jerusalem. The Temple was then looted and destroyed by the Babylonians in 586 BCE (2 Kgs. 25:8, 9, 13–17). The ark of the covenant, never mentioned again in the Old Testament, was gone. A second temple was constructed following the Babylonian exile. The temple called Herod's Temple began to be constructed around that temple, and this temple, destroyed in 70 AD, was the holy site of Jesus' time.

God lives among the people (Ex. 25:8; 29:45). When Jesus came, his followers understood *him* to be the glory of God, the special presence contained in the tabernacle and then the Temple. "We have seen his glory," writes John. God's glory and presence are "contained" in Jesus.

But to see God's glory in an everyday man? Not only that, but an everyday man who was once a baby, a child, at the Temple. As an adult, he met a tragic, shameful death, abandoned by nearly everyone and publically scorned. Do we see God's glory in him, as Simeon and Anna did, as the Apostle John did?

Yes. God may sometimes seem far off—and it's OK that we feel that way. Jesus' companions on the road to Emmaus felt the same way. But Christ was closer to them than they realized: in fact, he was right beside them. At Lent, we renew our sense of Christ's presence.

Prayer

Omnipresent Lord, we take for granted that you are always and readily available. Help us to have a lively and sensitive awareness that you "dwell among us" still and accompany us in all our ways. In your name we pray. Amen.

Digging Deeper

- The idea of "traveling mercies" comes from the days when Jews traveled to the Temple to worship. Read Psalm 121 and write down some ways you feel the Lord's presence when you're away from home.
- Consult a Bible dictionary and read more about the tabernacle and the temples.

Wednesday

The Messenger

Malachi 3:1–4; 4:5–6; Matthew 11:7–10

When I visited Israel years ago, I visited the Western Wall of the Temple and the Dome of the Rock, which stands on the Temple site. One site that really impressed me was the wilderness area south of Jerusalem, where Jesus' cousin John the Baptist had his ministry prior to Jesus' appearance. The prophet Malachi, who wrote centuries earlier, provided an indelible image both of John—the messenger who will "prepare the way"—and of Jesus—who will purify us like "a refiner's fire." (It is a music-worthy image, too, considering Handel's use of these words for his oratorio *Messiah*).

With words that harken to Isaiah 40:3–5, where the messenger is referred to as a wilderness voice, Malachi promises a preparer for the Lord's arrival (Mal. 3:1–4). In verses 5 and 6, he is identified with Elijah. Then the Lord himself will arrive. Imagine if Jesus discussed this passage with the two friends on the road to Emmaus, what a revelation they might have had, recognizing the similarity between John and the Elijah-like messenger Malachi foretold.

Malachi wrote during the time of the return from Babylonian exile. In about 586 BCE, the Babylonians had destroyed Jerusalem and carried God's people off into exile, but after about fifty years, many of the people returned to the land and began to rebuild Jerusalem and the Temple. These events, between 539 and the mid-400s BCE, are described in the biblical books of Ezra and Nehemiah. The people were especially eager to be faithful to God's covenant, for it was the sins of earlier generations that set in motion God's judgment against them, enacted through the conquering Babylonians. God is always faithful to his promises, though, and God promised to restore the people in their promised land.

But the Lord is a God who demands a holy, faithful people (Exod. 19:6). Malachi uses images of refinement. Gold is not harmed when melted, nor damaged in the refinement process, but the ore and other elements mixed with the gold are removed. Silver also must be refined in order to be pure and thus more valuable. Malachi also uses the image of cleaning new cloth in order to make it ready for use: the fuller's soap mentioned in verse 2 is a strong alkali used in the ancient production of clothing.

Altogether, these passages teach that believers are metaphorically purified in order to be holy. Lent is a time of turning and returning to God, of looking within our hearts to discern aspects of ourselves that are problematic, of asking God's Spirit to speak to us and guide us in our religious devotion. Beginning with Ash Wednesday, we face honestly our weakness and mortality, and we seek to retain a penitential, openhearted attitude during the Lenten weeks. It can be a meaningful time of refinement.

Many people undertake disciplines during Lent. They give up an everyday habit that they have counted on, that will require effort to abandon for forty days. You might consider no TV, no impulsive shopping, no reliance upon a food or drink that you turn to habitually. The absence of that favorite thing creates a void that reminds you to turn to and think about the Lord, and you grow in your reliance upon God. You also might do something that adds to rather than subtracts from your daily life, such as practicing kindness and forgiveness, serving the poor in some way, or attending additional religious services.

Lent is not a time of "leveraging" God through things we do or give up. We are not trying to convince God to love us via our extra efforts. Nor do we wallow in guilt when we fail. God already loves us more than we can ask or imagine. Lenten disciplines help us focus upon God's love that is already ours in abundance. Breaking out of our everyday habits, our everyday forgetfulness of God, helps us to seek the spiritual transformation that makes us more humble and more holy. We seek eagerly to be God's covenant people.

Prayer

Dear Lord, give me insight into ways you want me to be more holy. May my Lenten observance be meaningful, and may all the times of my life be opportunities for spiritual growth. Bless my church and the churches of my community. Amen.

Digging Deeper

Recall difficult times in your life. Did you discern God's care during these times? Was your faith hurt by the circumstances? If so, how are you still struggling to make sense of those times of difficulty? Keep asking the Lord to shelter you in divine care, and to help you see that care more clearly as time passes.

Thursday

The Voice in the Wilderness

Isaiah 40:3–5; Luke 3:2–17

Little kids get facts discombobulated. When I was a boy, I thought that John the Baptist was . . . Baptist, like one of the big churches in my small hometown. Fortunately, we talked about John the Baptist in my own church, and I soon learned about him: his baptism and his message.

Baptism is a Christian sacrament. Unlike other kinds of ritual washing, baptism is (in most denominations) done only once. That's because Christ does all the work for our salvation; there is no need to "redo" something that God has already done on our behalf. The corresponding rite of the Jewish covenant, circumcision, was of course done only once, for baby boys.

John the Baptist fulfills a passage from Isaiah. This is one of those Old Testament passages that inspire me to hum along with the words because Handel set them so beautifully in his *Messiah*.

> A voice cries out:
> "In the wilderness prepare the way of the LORD,
>   make straight in the desert a highway for our God.
> Every valley shall be lifted up,
>   and every mountain and hill be made low;
> the uneven ground shall become level,
>   and the rough places a plain.
> Then the glory of the LORD shall be revealed,
>   and all people shall see it together,
>   for the mouth of the LORD has spoken."

In Isaiah's vision, the Lord is on the way. It's joyful news, for the people were lost in exile and despair, but now the Lord is coming! Through the rugged and uneven territory, the way before the Lord will be made smooth and easy.

24

In Isaiah, the voice is unidentified. Perhaps it is a figurative, poetic image drawn for the real-life practice of a herald announcing the ruler's arrival. In their Gospels, Mark and Matthew right away identify the announcer as John the Baptist, with Jesus making the same identification in Matthew 11:10 and Luke 7:27. In his Gospel, Luke gives much more background on John's parents, Zechariah and Elizabeth, including the lovely story of Mary's journey to visit Elizabeth.

John has helped my faith tremendously in a particular regard. Read about John's ministry in Luke 3:10–14:

> And the crowds asked him, "What then should we do?" In reply he said to them, "Whoever has two coats must share with anyone who has none; and whoever has food must do likewise." Even tax collectors came to be baptized, and they asked him, "Teacher, what should we do?" He said to them, "Collect no more than the amount prescribed for you." Soldiers also asked him, "And we, what should we do?" He said to them, "Do not extort money from anyone by threats or false accusation, and be satisfied with your wages."

In our eagerness to please the Lord, we may think we should be involved in many kinds of ministries. Then we become involved in too many, and we become discouraged that we can't do enough. The world has so many problems, and we despair about making any difference. But John tells people: do the small but important things that you can do. Make the changes in your life that are possible now. Good advice as we examine our spiritual lives during this Lenten season.

Many artists have depicted John the Baptist: da Vinci, Raphael, Titian, Caravaggio, and others. One of my favorites is Matthias Grünewald's "Isenheim Altarpiece." John stands to the side of the crucified Jesus and points his finger at the anguished Lord. John died prior to Jesus, so to place him at the crucifixion is symbolic rather than historical. But the symbolism is apt, because that was John's inspiring ministry: to stand to the side and direct our attention to the Messiah.

Perhaps, in explaining the scriptural meaning of John the Baptist to his two walking companions, Jesus remembered the last time he and his relative met, along the waters of the Jordan.

Prayer

Dear Lord, repentance is difficult. And yet, we are in a better situation than John's original hearers: we know the truth to which he pointed. Guide us in seeking your presence more fully, not from fear but from love and joy. In Christ's name. Amen.

Digging Deeper

- The prophet Elijah (who did not die: 2 Kgs. 2:11) was long associated with the coming of the Messiah (Mal. 4:5–6). Jesus connects Elijah and John the Baptist in Matthew 11:7–14, although John himself denied the identity (John 1:19–23). Read about Elijah in a Bible dictionary or online site. Why was he significant?
- How much service-related activity do you incorporate into your life? Are there opportunities to take on (or put aside) during this Lenten season?

Friday

Jesus' Baptism in the Jordan

Psalm 114; Micah 6:4–5; Matthew 3:13–17

When I visited the Holy Land, I purchased a small vial of water from the River Jordan. It is closed with a wooden cap topped with a cross. It is a nice reminder of a visit to a river that is much smaller than I'd expected. From all the hymns I had ever heard (like "Roll, Jordan, Roll") I had expected something as mighty as the Mississippi or the Ohio.

But the river has tremendous significance in biblical history. Water is frequently a symbol of God's life and of God's rescue. God's splitting of the sea in Exodus is one of the most momentous events of Scripture, but read Joshua 3–4 and you'll also see how momentous is God's splitting of the Jordan River, when the people ended the forty years in the wilderness and arrived at the promised land. The stories of the Bible had been building toward this moment: all the years Moses had led the people were aimed at getting the people to this point. Even before that, God had promised Abraham that his descendants would be many and that they would live on the land. Now they were here—and the river split so they could cross on dry land. The short Psalm 114 connects the God of creation with the exodus and with the crossing of the Jordan.

The location on the west side of the Jordan, to which the Israelites crossed, was called Gilgal. This is where the people first encamped, after leaving the place called Shittim. Micah 6:4–5 alludes to the crossing of the Jordan and links it with God's great, saving acts. It is also the place where Elijah crossed the Jordan just before he was taken up in a whirlwind (2 Kgs. 2:1–12).[3] This incident led to another popular image from "old time" hymns: that of crossing the Jordan meaning being with the Lord forever.

Gilgal was also the place where Samuel anointed Saul as king but then rejected Saul, setting the stage for David (1 Sam.

27

11:14–15; 13:8–15). Jesus, *the* Anointed One, is baptized near the place associated with the beginning of the Israelite monarchy. So the Jordan is ripe with biblical connections: Abraham, Moses, Joshua, and Jesus; David and Jesus; John the Baptist and Elijah.

Jesus might have been baptized any place, but when he went to the Jordan for baptism, he tacitly acknowledged his people's long history with God's salvation.

"Then Jesus came from Galilee to John at the Jordan, to be baptized by him" (Matt. 3:13). This is a shock. John had always warned people about the one who would soon bring the kingdom of heaven: though John baptized for repentance, he who was to come would baptize with the Spirit and with fire, rescuing some and damning others. But like Jesus' birth, his arrival at the Jordan is without fanfare, certainly without wrath and fire. John himself was taken aback.

He asked the question we all ask: Why did Jesus seek baptism?

Jesus underwent baptism in order to identify with people like you and me.

Baptism is the beginning of his journey to redeem sinners. His journey led him to the cross, the quintessential place where he identified with suffering, sinful humanity.

Jesus said he had to be baptized in order to "fulfill all righteousness." Righteousness (*tzedakah* in Hebrew) means steadfastness, faithfulness, integrity, and justice. God's righteousness is shown in God's desire to save sinners and be in a relationship with sinners. When Jesus said that this was the purpose of his baptism, he meant that God is working in and through him (Jesus) to rescue (save) us and bless us.

Jesus did God's will, to fulfill the righteousness of God, or in other words, to fulfill the way God takes the side of sinners. Thus Jesus went to be baptized.

Prayer

Lord of life, who waded into the Jordan River, no one has taken my side the way you did. During this Lenten season, I ask that you take my side in these ways that I name in my heart today. Thank you. Amen.

Digging Deeper

- Read aloud Romans 3:21–26, where Paul assures his readers that God's righteousness is revealed in the way God saves sinners. Consider memorizing this passage for your Lenten devotion and beyond.
- What was your baptism like? What does baptism mean to you? Look in a hymnal and, if there is a service of baptism there, think about its meanings.
- Get a Bible dictionary and study the different ways the Jordan River figured in biblical history.

Saturday

The Temptation of Jesus

Deuteronomy 6:4–9; 6:16; 8:3; Matthew 4:1–11

Are you fasting during Lent or giving up something that you enjoy as a spiritual discipline?

Because of the way some Bible editions are divided into sections, we might miss the relationship among stories and teachings. The story of Jesus' temptation is an example. In his baptism, Jesus shows himself as willing to do God's will in order to fulfill God's righteousness: in other words, to fulfill God's plan of salvation. The temptation story is the next stage, a more dire stage, building upon that baptismal obedience (Matt. 4:1–11; Mark 1:12–13; Luke 4:1–13).

Jesus goes into the wilderness region, the inhospitable Judean desert. The stories say he fasts there for forty days. The number "forty" is a biblical number for a time of hardship: for instance, the Israelites' forty years in the wilderness (Num. 14:34; Deut. 8:2; Ps. 95:10; and others).

"Wilderness," too, is a biblical theme. Today we think of wilderness as natural areas that we need to protect from development, regions that people can enjoy for their natural beauty. In the Bible, "wilderness" is an area (and a time) of testing and difficulty but also possibly a time of drawing closer to God.

If you're like me, you have moments when you feel like you're not as strong as other times, when you're not your best. I don't like having to make important decisions when I'm very tired, for instance. Jesus was alone and ascetic for nearly six weeks, and he was vulnerable. Sure enough, this was the time when he had to deal with the tempter.

Although the text doesn't allude to Genesis 3, in a strong way this story fulfills the story of Adam and Eve and the serpent. As in the garden of Eden, the questioner tried to instill doubt about what God wanted. But unlike Jesus' (and our) ancestors in

Eden, Jesus did not succumb; he reversed that first sin and thus continued to fulfill God's plan of salvation. Jesus was the Son of God (Ps. 2:7; Luke 1:32–33), but the tempter said, "If you are the Son of God, command these stones to become loaves of bread." Rather than be doubtful because of that "if," Jesus responded with a portion of Deuteronomy 8:3, "One does not live by bread alone." The whole verse is a reminder to the Israelites of how God sustained them in the wilderness, providing them bread, and that bread came forth from the power and word of God.

Then Jesus returned to the city with the tempter saying, in effect, "Look, Jesus, here is a high place. If you're God's Son, jump, and you'll see how the Lord will protect you." Satan even quoted a psalm, 91:11–12, in order to show to Jesus that Scripture promises protection. But again, Satan did not fool or mislead Jesus, who responded with yet another Scripture, partially quoting Deuteronomy 6:16, "Do not put the LORD your God to the test."

Then the tempter gave him a vision of the world's kingdoms, and the "if" became conditional: "All these I will give you, if you will fall down and worship me." Quoting from Deuteronomy 6:13, Jesus was firm and dismissive: "Worship the Lord your God, and serve only him" (Matt. 4:10).

With that, the devil left Jesus, but not forever. In a story arc, Jesus faced another horrible challenge when he was rejected and vulnerable during his final hours (Matt. 27:40–43).[4] In that different circumstance, Jesus fulfilled Scripture by remaining silent before his accusers (Isa. 53:7).

I like to think of this story, not as an example of how we should have greater will power, but as a story of who Jesus is. He went through the water, entered the wilderness, felt weak and vulnerable, yet, unlike his ancestors, he did not fall prey. He remained obedient to God's plan of salvation, of which you and I are 24/7 beneficiaries.

Prayer
Holy Trinity, help me withstand temptations that are vexing me today. Give me the strength and direction to overcome the difficult things I'm dealing with today. Amen.

Digging Deeper

- How are you tempted? What temptations are the most difficult for you to withstand? Does it help to know Jesus was too? Is resisting temptation a matter of will power, or of drawing closer to Christ, or both?
- What in your life qualifies as a "wilderness experience," that is, a time of uncertainty and anxiety when your faith was tested?

Second Sunday Reflection

The stories of John's call to repentance and of Jesus' wilderness temptations remind us that Lent is a traditional time of self-examination and self-denial. We would not undertake the extreme self-denial of Jesus in the wilderness. But we might give up something we like for the forty days or, with a doctor's permission, we might fast for short periods. An alternative would be to take up a task that is sacrificial, like volunteering at a local ministry.

Repentance (*teshuvah* in Hebrew) is a turning away from things in our lives that hinder our relationship to God and, simultaneously, it is a turning back to God. Actions of self-denial and service help facilitate our turning back.

Are these ways to earn God's favor or to leverage God to help us? It's easy for us to start thinking that way: "Dear Lord, if I give up chocolate or sex or swearing, would you help me find a new job?" But we need never try to convince God to help us, to earn God's love, because we already have God's love in abundance. That old hymn "How Firm a Foundation," harkening to Jesus' experience in the wilderness, is a beautiful reminder of his unearned faithfulness:

> The soul that on Jesus doth lean for repose,
> I will not, I will not, desert to his foes;
> That soul, though all hell should endeavor to shake,
> I'll never, no never, no never forsake.

That's a beautiful thing that I take from this week's stories of Jesus. They're stories of Jesus doing all the things necessary to gain for us God's mercies and salvation.

Observing Lent helps us grow in our relationship with God

to keep the relationship fresh and vital from our side. As with any relationship, our faith has to be nourished and sustained. If you have a dear friend, the friendship will eventually wither if you neglect your friend and fall out of touch (though your friend may still love you). So we focus upon Jesus, his life and his saving work.

Jesus is our dear companion for all of life's journeys.

Prayer

Dear Lord, I know that you are always close to me. But many days I don't feel it. There have been times in my life when I wondered where you were. I need renewal, a fresh start. Help me know that you always love me, cherish me, take my side, and give me life. Amen.

Digging Deeper

What disciplines are you doing this Lenten season, if any? Do you think that they help you? What are some practices you can begin to help you feel closer to God?

Monday

Jesus Begins His Ministry

Isaiah 9:1–7; Matthew 4:12–17

In Matthew's Gospel (4:12–17), Jesus begins his ministry after he learns of the arrest of John the Baptist. Jesus leaves Nazareth and withdraws to Galilee.

> He . . . made his home in Capernaum by the lake, in the territory of Zebulun and Naphtali, so that what had been spoken through the prophet Isaiah might be fulfilled: "Land of Zebulun, land of Naphtali, on the road by the sea, across the Jordan, Galilee of the Gentiles—the people who sat in darkness have seen a great light, and for those who sat in the region and shadow of death light has dawned."
>
> From that time Jesus began to proclaim, 'Repent, for the kingdom of heaven has come near.'" (Matt. 4:13–17)

Matthew quotes the first part of the Isaiah passage that we studied earlier: Isaiah 9:1–7. The passage refers to Zebulun, the Israelite tribe associated with the Galilee area of Nazareth, and also Naphtali, the tribe associated with the Galilee area where Capernaum was located. But Galilee also had a significant Gentile population, so the passage refers to both Jews and non-Jews blessed by the coming king.

Matthew understood the beginning of Jesus' ministry—even

his home base—as a fulfillment of Scripture. Galilee is honored in a similar way as Bethlehem.

Isaiah lived in the northern kingdom during difficult times. This poem probably dates from the time of the Syro-Ephraimite war (about 734 BCE), and the original context was likely the birth of a crown prince in the royal family, or possibly a verse for the coronation of King Hezekiah (727 BCE).[1]

We know what it's like to be a nation at war. It is a time of darkness, and it's hard to see the light at the end. Families are broken up, people are injured or killed, and the national mood is one of distress. Warfare was of course different in the Iron Age of the ancient Near East compared to today, but the human cost of war is always high. Indeed, the northern kingdom (Ephraim) fell to the Assyrians in about 722 BCE and never recovered.

So the birth of a royal child, or the ascension of a new leader, was cause for rejoicing. It was a time of light through darkness, so wonderful that even the very land of Galilee will be honored. Read the whole passage from Isaiah again, and you will see how joyous will be the end of war, the burning of military garments, and well-being for the people. The new leader will grow in authority, will bring unending peace, and will uphold justice and righteousness "from that time on and forever." The dynasty of David will endure. No mere mortal could do all this, but rather "the zeal of the Lord Almighty."

Jesus was not a baby by this point. But he came bearing a message of peace and justice that brought hope to people living under military occupation and foreign government. The kingdom is on the way. He began preaching with the authority predicted in our Isaiah passage. At the end of Matthew's Gospel (28:18), the risen Christ announces that authority.

Jesus' message had deeper meanings yet than a strong historical dynasty, important as that was. We'll see in tomorrow's lesson that Jesus announced a kingdom of peace for Jews and Gentiles alike. But repentance is necessary, that crucial turning toward God so that people can know and recognize the kingdom as it comes near.

Prayer

Dear Lord Jesus, did you have feelings of anticipation and uncertainty as you began your ministry? Did you have a clear and confident sense of purpose? Or did you experience a combination of feelings? Be with me (and my own complicated emotions) as I go about my life's tasks and embark on new beginnings. Amen.

Digging Deeper

- Think of times when you began a new job, moved to a new location, or otherwise began a new chapter in your life. How did it turn out? How did you seek God's guidance beforehand (if at all)?
- Think about repentance. Have there been times when you felt deeply repentant about something? If so, what did you do? How did the experience affect your relationship with God? During Lent, are you repentant about any particular thing?

Tuesday

Jesus in the Synagogue

Isaiah 61:1–2; Isaiah 58:6; Luke 4:16–30

During this Lent, think about how you feel toward people who are different from you. Many of us struggle with feelings of prejudice or disdain or animosity. We're unsure about people who aren't like us. These attitudes are deeply engrained in us, and even when we want to change, we find it difficult.

In this story near the beginning of Luke, Jesus is engaged in Scripture study at the synagogue. Jesus took the scroll and read a passage from Isaiah 61:1–2. The original passage, which Luke has edited (including the insertion of Isaiah 58:6), reads:

> The spirit of the Lord GOD is upon me,
> because the LORD has anointed me;
> he has sent me to bring good news to the oppressed,
> to bind up the brokenhearted,
> to proclaim liberty to the captives,
> and release to the prisoners;
> to proclaim the year of the Lord's favor,
> and the day of vengeance of our God.

Jesus' omission of that last verse is significant, for this was not the time of "vengeance" but of ministry to those who are in need.

In the liturgy of the Lord's Supper, we pray the words, "pour out your Holy Spirit." In biblical times, anointing a guest with scented oil was a sign of respect and hospitality (Ps. 23 refers to the custom), but anointing was also a ceremony for the high priest, or for a new king. Exodus 20:22–33 refers to the anointing of the high priests and the utensils of the tabernacle. The word "messiah" (not quoted here in Isaiah) means "one who has been anointed," but it came to refer to God's eventual deliverer, anointed by God's Spirit.

Jesus read the passage and then he sat down; after a dramatic pause, he announced the fulfillment of the passage. The men were impressed at his words and knew that his background was from a working Nazareth family.

Then Jesus turned more provocative. On one level, he knew that the "hometown folk" would automatically question things he said and did. They "knew him when," as the saying goes. But he explained the Scripture to show the broadness of God's work. As you read the Luke passage, understand that the people to whom Jesus alluded were Gentiles. One is the story of Elijah, who was sent into Gentile territory (Zarephath in Sidon) and brought to life the dead son of the widow (1 Kgs. 17:17–24). Jesus also alludes to the story of Elisha, who healed lepers, including the Gentile Naaman (2 Kgs. 5:1–9). Basically Jesus was saying that God is in the process of fulfilling these Scriptures, but in a way that involves Gentiles, and thus God will show favor to people both within and outside God's own people. God's mercy is unlimited.

To be fair, God's people had suffered under the oppression and hostility of Gentiles for a long time. We have the benefit of hindsight; but Jesus' contemporaries were tired of decades of military occupation. They became so distressed that they drove him out of town and even hoped to toss him off a cliff. In matters of religion, things do become ugly very quickly.

Without going into detail, Luke writes that Jesus slipped through the crowd and went on his way.

But what a beautiful vision Jesus presented! The God-sized, inclusive love that doesn't take sides or impose boundaries, the love that deeply helps people who need help most, love that provides real, tangible help. It's the love that Jesus also expressed in the Beatitudes: how blessed are those who are in need, who long for righteousness and for comfort. God is with them and for them.

Prayer

Lord Jesus, you abolished barriers between people, and we persist in raising them up. As we take this Lenten walk with you, we thank you for identifying places in our hearts that still need your transforming grace. Amen.

Digging Deeper

- How do you "process" rejection? Imagine a scale of 1 to 10, with "1" being that you brush off rejection quickly and "10" being that it makes you deeply depressed for a long time. Where are you on that scale? (I'm about a 7.)
- Read the Beatitudes (Matt. 5:3–11). How do they fit within Jesus' vision of blessedness and liberation?

Wednesday

Teaching in Parables

Psalm 78:2–3; Isaiah 6:9–10; Matthew 13:10–17; 34–35

I teach college classes in history, philosophy, and religion. I love teaching, and my students are wonderful. Once in a while, I have to repeat the same point over and over. The other day, after I discussed the required length and due date of the research paper, a student raised a hand and asked, "When is the paper due? How long does it have to be?" It does no good to get impatient with students, but sometimes I shake my head. I miss key information, too, sometimes.

Learning has a component of readiness. If you're not ready to learn, the teacher can be wonderful, but you won't learn. When you're ready, things become clear.

A parable is a story, an analogy that teaches a principle or a lesson. The Old Testament contains a few parables. Nathan told David a parable of a rich man who killed a poor man's lamb (2 Sam. 12:1–4). Another parable is found in Isaiah 5:1–7, a story of a vineyard wherein the vineyard was Israel.

Jesus frequently taught in parables, especially as recorded in the Synoptic Gospels (Matthew, Mark, and Luke). Well-known parables include the lost sheep, the lost coin, the Prodigal Son, the Good Samaritan, and others. At some point in your spiritual journey, study the parables on your own, if you haven't already.

Usually Jesus' parables make use of some recognizable aspect of everyday life. Anyone could understand the desperation of looking for something important that is missing, or worrying about one special person even though everyone else in your life is fine, or feeling both compassion and caution when you see someone in need along the road or the street.

Many of the parables refer to the kingdom of God (or kingdom of heaven). In other words, they teach about the time when God will rule, but since God is always understood as Israel's true

41

monarch, the kingdom of which Jesus teaches points to a time when God will rule in a new and fresh way. The parables encourage people to recognize the coming kingdom and to heed Jesus' teachings. They also warn people of the foolishness of missing the signs of the kingdom.

Jesus' parables are unique in this kind of literature, because they refer to *himself.* They equate Jesus' ministry with God's saving work.[2] Also, they implicitly apply various titles of God to Jesus: the Sower, the Rock, the Shepherd, the Bridegroom, the Father, the Lord, and the King. Old Testament parables were not messianic in reference, but Jesus' certainly were.[3]

In the parallel Scriptures Matthew 13:10–15, Mark 4:10–12, and Luke 8:9–10, Jesus explains his use of parables: to fulfill the Scriptures that people will listen and hear but not understand. That seems discouraging: Why would Jesus (or God speaking through the prophet Isaiah) want people to miss the point? As the footnote in my Bible indicates, if people wanted to get the point, they could just ask Jesus. That's what his disciples did. But for others, a lack of understanding meant a lack of engagement or of readiness to learn.

Jesus was low-key about his messianic identity. Otherwise he might be swept up in a popular movement that misrepresented his purposes. But he taught the deep and wonderful love of God through memorable stories and similes, and at the same time he taught that he himself was a new and wondrous work of God. Anytime you're blue about your spiritual life, for instance, just read the parable of the Prodigal Son; there, you read about God's attitude toward you and me.

Prayer

Teacher Jesus, open our ears, hearts, and minds that we might understand those things you want us to know. Be patient as we struggle toward a strong faith and a deeper knowledge. Be patient when we are slow to understand. Amen.

Digging Deeper
- Think of a time when you misunderstood something important or when you were misunderstood.
- Do you like to teach? If so, how would you describe your teaching style?
- Who was your favorite teacher (in school or in church)?

Thursday

The Kingdom

2 Samuel 7:16; Isaiah 9:7; Luke 17:20–21

"Thy Kingdom come, Thy will be done," we pray Sunday after Sunday (Matt. 6:10; Luke 11:2), and maybe on other days of the week, too.

We have already thought about Jesus' identity as king, but there is more. The theme of so many of Jesus' parables was the kingdom of God, or the kingdom of heaven. The phrase itself is not used in the Old Testament, but the sovereignty of God over his people is a major theme; God leads his people and works out the divine purposes in and through his people. In the New Testament, Jesus is newly understood to be the fulfillment of God's purposes in the monarchy. In the parables and other conversations, Jesus refers to himself as the Son of Man, a figure in Daniel 7 that came to be interpreted as the Messiah.

Jesus is not a conventional monarch, though. Pilate mocked Jewish hopes of rescue from Gentile oppression when he charged Jesus with being "King of the Jews" (John 19:19). In other words, this sorry, rejected, executed man represented Roman contempt for what they considered a troublesome people. But Jesus' followers affirmed that he was indeed sovereign—that his cross was his "throne." His cross was part of God's plan for Christ's resurrection and thus Christ's kingly authority over sin, evil, and death.

If the kingdom has a crucified king, what is the kingdom? It is certainly not a geographic location, nor an institution, including the institutional church. As good as institutions can be, they are fallible and self-protecting, just like individuals. God's rule is greater than any human organization. We see this aspect of the kingdom in Jesus' teachings. Organizations have employees and members, and with those, qualification. In Jesus' teachings, the "wrong," even unqualified people seem to be able to belong to the kingdom (e.g., Matt. 21:31).

The kingdom is not a social program that we structure in order to change society. True, God demands obedience in the social world. But we ourselves cannot "build" the kingdom through, for instance, government legislation and political action. Again, God's rule is greater than even our sincere efforts to follow Christ's teachings in society.

God's rule is connected to God's love. In Luke 17:20–21, we read: "Once Jesus was asked by the Pharisees when the kingdom of God was coming, and he answered, 'The kingdom of God is not coming with things that can be observed; nor will they say, "Look, here it is!" or "There it is!" For, in fact, the kingdom of God is among you.'" The Greek word for "among" can also mean "within." Imagine the kingdom of God being within people's hearts but also among the people who seek to show God's loving-kindness to the world in Jesus' name.

The kingdom is a dynamic thing. Jesus warned that people could "miss" the kingdom—the opportunity will come and then go. In other words, the kingdom is linked to Jesus himself, and people in his own time missed his significance (Matt. 5:20; 7:21; 19:23–24; and others).

But Jesus' identity could be missed because he was so different from what one could consider a royal personage. The kingdom is related to God's authority over life and death.

Explaining the Scriptures to the friends going to Emmaus, the risen Christ told them of the necessity of the sufferings of the Messiah (Luke 24:26). The power and glory that one would associate with the establishment of a divine kingdom is first shown in the very unroyal sufferings of Christ and then in the power that rescues us for eternal life.

Prayer
Dear Lord, help us to have a sense of proximity to your kingdom, especially in the form of loving-kindness from others whom we know. Amen.

Digging Deeper

- Do you fear death? Have you had "brushes" with death? How do Jesus' teachings about the kingdom help your feelings about death?
- The city of Jerusalem is symbolic of the well-being of the people (Luke 2:39). Look up Jerusalem in a Bible dictionary and think about its significance.

Friday

The Great Commandments

Deuteronomy 6:4–9; Leviticus 19:18; Mark 12:28–34

Ever since reading the novels of Chaim Potok for a college freshman class in religion, I've always been fascinated by Jewish devotion to Torah study. Psalms like 19 and 119 extoll God's beautiful law. But we Christians don't often read the Torah laws in a devotional, searching way, as many Jews do.

Jesus was a teacher of Jewish law and traditions. The Laws of the Torah (the Bible's first five books) are traditionally numbered at 613. In different times of Jewish history, including Jesus' time, there have been discussions on how to summarize the laws. For instance, the Rabbi Hillel, who died when Jesus was a child, was asked to summarize the Law, and he responded, "What is hateful to yourself, do not do to your fellow man. That is the whole Torah; the rest is just commentary. Go and study it."[4] In Mark 12:28–34, the Law expert who speaks with Jesus reflected that same interest. He and Jesus agreed on the two most important ones: Deuteronomy 6:4 and Leviticus 19:18.

Deuteronomy 6:4–9 is a classic passage, still precious, recited, and taken to heart among Jews.

> Hear, O Israel: The LORD is our God, the LORD alone. You shall love the LORD your God with all your heart, and with all your soul, and with all your might. Keep these words that I am commanding you today in your heart. Recite them to your children and talk about them when you are at home and when you are away, when you lie down and when you rise. Bind them as a sign on your hand, fix them as an emblem on your forehead, and write them on the doorposts of your house and on your gates.

Leviticus 19:18 is another important passage within the Torah:

"You shall not take vengeance or bear a grudge against any of your people, but you shall love your neighbor as yourself: I am the LORD." This and the Deuteronomy passage represent two sides to the believer's daily life of faith: to love God with one's whole person, so to speak, and to love other people. 1 John 4:7–21 reiterates that dual love: we cannot love God and hate each other, for otherwise, we lie when we say we love God.

Love is an easy thing to say, more difficult to do. We all have known people who say they love someone but really don't mean it, or their love is so conditional or unreliable as to be false. The Hebrew word translated as "steadfast love" or "loving-kindness" is *hesed*. God loves in that kind of way: ongoing, kind, unfailing, and faithful to God's covenant.

One's neighbor can and should be anyone. In Judaism, acts of service to Jews and Gentiles alike are a strong aspect of religious faith; given the choice between formal religious observance and an act of service and helpfulness, the faithful Jew will always choose service and good deeds. Jesus is very much teaching his own religious faith to us Gentiles.

We can deepen our understanding of Gospel passages by seeing what stories are before and after. In Luke's Gospel, the exchange between the legal scholar and Jesus serves as an introduction to two stories: Jesus' parable of the Good Samaritan, and the story of Jesus, Mary, and Martha. The Good Samaritan actively loved his neighbor, regardless of the fact that his neighbor was someone of a different religious and ethnic demographic than he. Mary actively loved God by, in this case, not doing anything but listening to Jesus.

There are two sides to loving, and they cannot be separated. Not just learning about Jesus, but being with Jesus, is the source of our ability to love one another.

Prayer

Lord God, I confess that I haven't loved you with my whole heart, and I have people in my life whom I not only do not love but also deeply dislike. Be with me in my life to show me ways my heart can become ever more open to the wellsprings of your love. Amen.

Digging Deeper

Do you ever get discouraged by Christians who don't love, or who say they love but they don't really seem to? What are ways in which Christians (you and I, too) can grow in love?

Saturday

Greater Prophet

Deuteronomy 18:19–21; John 7:40–41

In the Emmaus story, Cleopas refers to Jesus as "a prophet mighty in deed and word." I have known Christians who were quick to stress that Jesus was more than a prophet. And yet, during his life, Jesus was frequently understood to be a prophet (Matt. 21:11; Mark 6:15; 8:28; Luke 7:16; John 4:19; 6:14; Acts 2:30). He possessed the Spirit in a way that people considered prophetic (Matt. 12:28; Luke 1:76–77; 4:18–20; 22:64). He elicited people's excitement as a prophet.

That's because Moses foretold a great prophet (Deut.18:15–18), and the Hebrew people longed for a great prophet, perhaps as eagerly as they anticipated a Davidic king, as reflected in our passage, John 7:40–41, as well as John 6:14. The Samaritan woman in John 4 declared that Jesus was Messiah and Prophet.

Who are prophets? They are people who have been divinely inspired to speak God's words or to speak on behalf of God. Fifty-five prophets are listed in the Old Testament, including seven women (Sarah, Miriam, Deborah, Hannah, Abigail, Huldah, and Esther).[5] Of these fifty-five prophets, sixteen (Isaiah through Malachi) have biblical books. If you read these books, you see how the prophets spoke to God's people and sometimes to neighboring nations. The prophets issued warnings and judgments against the people's sins, their idolatry and lack of justice, but also offered promises for the future and words of assurance. They stressed that justice, righteousness, mercy, and faithfulness to the covenant must go hand in hand with religious worship. The prophets deal with issues important for the people: God's promises back to Abraham, the promised land, the covenant, the failures of the monarchy, and the Temple (and, in Jeremiah and Ezekiel, its loss).

In Jewish understanding, Moses is the greatest of all the prophets. "Never since has there arisen a prophet in Israel like

Moses, whom the LORD knew face to face" (Deut. 34:10). The Lord declared:

> When there are prophets among you,
>> I the LORD make myself known to them in visions;
>> I speak to them in dreams.
> Not so with my servant Moses;
>> he is entrusted with all my house.
> With him I speak face to face—
>> clearly, not in riddles;
>> and he beholds the form of the LORD.
>
> (Num. 12:6–8)

New Testament writers preached the primacy of Christ; in Christ, God has revealed the purpose and goal of salvation and has revealed a new attitude toward the Law (Heb. 3:1–6). Thus, Moses seems undervalued in the New Testament. But what a tremendous figure of intercessory love and compassion. He takes the side of the people, stands up for them, suffers on their behalf, and refuses to allow God to wipe them out (Exod. 32:11–14). To expect a prophet on par with Moses is to expect someone very special.

Jesus' role as prophet differed in a key way from other prophets. Although other Old Testament prophets injected their own personalities, sadness, distress, and feelings into their message, nevertheless they spoke primarily on behalf of God, expressing the will of God. Jesus expressed the will of God, but as is the case of the parables, his message referred to his own unity with God. That's different than simply injecting his own personality into his message.

Moses tells the people that God will always provide for them, in terms of their physical needs but also their spiritual ones. God's great prophet will come, and the truth of his message can be verified and validated. The truth of Jesus' message was verified and validated by his eventual death and resurrection.

Prayer

Lord Christ, people looked to you as someone who would speak with authority about God. Today, we know that you speak for

God and that you are God's Son to show us the way. Stay with us and speak to us. Amen.

Digging Deeper

You may know the line from Simon and Garfunkel's song, "The Sounds of Silence": "The words of the prophets are written on the subway walls and tenement halls." Are there prophets today? If so, who are they, in your opinion? Is there power of prophecy in our own time?

Third Sunday Reflection

Say your own name to yourself. It is a way people identify you and know you. Withholding or changing your whole name has the effect of concealing or erasing your past. A famous western novel, *The Virginian* by Owen Wister, chronicled the adventures of a cowboy depicted as a good man, but he is a mystery because his actual name is not revealed.

A change of name can be a new beginning. I read an article recently about immigrant families who "Americanized" their names in order to fit in better with society and also to "move on" from their difficult earlier lives. A new name is a fresh start.

Name changes in the Bible had that quality. Think of Jacob, who became Israel. Abram and Sarai became Abraham and Sarah. Simon became Peter, the rock. Saul became known by his Roman name, Paul, as he preached around the Roman Empire.

Another aspect of identity is your place of origin. I like for people to know I'm from Vandalia (Fayette County), Illinois. My family roots are there, many friendships, and many of my interests (including Bible study) began there.

The Bible is a story of God's "roots," so to speak. When God appeared to Moses in the burning bush, he told Moses his name (Exod. 3:13–15). Now, we know God because the name of God is associated with the amazing things God has done. God became associated with his people; God invested his name in their well-being and their history, in a particular place (Num. 6:27). Jews often use the term *HaShem*, "the Name," when referring to God.

As we've seen this week, Jesus' teachings and actions pointed to God but also pointed to his own identity with God. Jesus' followers, consequently, became known because of Jesus. For instance, in Acts 4, Peter declares his faithfulness to the name of Jesus Christ of Nazareth and says that "There is salvation in no one else, for there is no other name under heaven given among mortals by which we must be saved" (Acts 4:12).

This week, we have thought about Jesus in terms of his identity as a teacher, Messiah, prophet, and also a resident of Galilee. These are ways that we, too, get to know Jesus more deeply—not as a character in a book, but as a living Lord who is with us at this moment.

Prayer

Dear Lord, each of us is different and comes from different places, and you love who we are and where we're from. Continue to help us draw closer to you. In the name of the Father, Son, and Holy Spirit. Amen.

Digging Deeper

Write down all the things you associate with your own name: relatives whom you were named for, the people who named you, the national origins of your surname, and so on. Think of these as ways God cherishes you as an individual whom God loves.

Monday

Power to Heal

Isaiah 53:4; Hosea 5:15–6:6; Matthew 8:16–17; Matthew 9:10–13

A re you dealing with any diseases or medical problems during this Lenten season? Last summer, I had to undergo medical tests. The symptom turned out to indicate nothing, but I worried and prayed for a month. Some of my friends are dealing with serious illness. We all face periods in our lives when we deal with medical issues. They are faith-testing times, wilderness times.

Jesus healed a number of people: a woman with a chronic hemorrhage, people unable to walk, blind people, people with leprosy (a term which covers a range of serious skin conditions), and people who were demon possessed. He healed many more whose stories are not recorded (Matt. 8:16–17; Mark 1:34; Luke 4:40).

As Jesus walked and talked en route to Emmaus, he might have mentioned the Messiah's many healing miracles and talked about God's concern for people's health and peace (Isa. 35:3–6). For instance, in Psalm 103:3, where the Lord is the one "who forgives all your iniquity, who heals all your diseases." And in Psalm 30, the gravely ill psalmist reasons with God then rejoices at God's care.

Jesus' healings were also signs of the kingdom of heaven. The healing miracles showed the people that God was at work in the life of Jesus—and they would understand even more about the saving power of God when Jesus later rose from the dead.

Today's Old Testament passages gather together these realities

55

from several directions. In our reading, Matthew 8:16–17, the Gospel author cites Isaiah 53:4. Understood as a fulfilled prophecy, the Isaiah passage tells of the servant of God who suffers dreadfully and, in fact, dies from the abuse. But through God's plan of salvation, the servant's suffering confers healing and well-being to the people.

In Matthew 9:10–13, the Pharisees disliked the fact that Jesus sat with "tax collectors and sinners." Jesus says to them, "Go and learn what this means, 'I desire mercy, not sacrifice.' For I have come to call not the righteous but sinners" (v. 13).

The whole passage from Hosea, 5:15–6:6, uses language of sickness and wellness (rising from one's sick bed) to refer to repentance. But also, the reference to "the third day" (Hos. 6:2) calls attention to Exodus 19:11, 15, wherein God establishes his Sinai covenant on the third day. So these words of Jesus connect his miracles and compassion, with the mercy that God demands of us, and also with Jesus' resurrection on the third day, which is a part of the new covenant. But that new covenant is also based upon Jesus' redemptive suffering, interpreted via the Isaiah passage.[1]

Divine healing can be a difficult subject. If I am sick and call upon Christ, and if I am not thereby healed, does Jesus not love me? Am I being punished for something?

Jesus' healings did not prolong people's physical lives indefinitely. The fact that we will someday have diseases that are not cured does not mean that Jesus loves us one ounce less. The Greek word *sozo* means both "to heal" and "to save." We affirm Jesus' saving power over all our lives, leading us to everlasting life, whether or not our physical diseases are cured.

The objections of the Pharisees in that passage alert us to another aspect: Jesus' healing was not just physical, for he also aimed to heal people of their hardness of heart or their metaphorical blindness. We may think that our physical diseases are more urgent than our spiritual "sicknesses," such as our prejudices, our grudges, our lack of love, and so on. But not necessarily. Jesus offers us the chance to be healed of these things, too.

What aspects of ourselves cry out for healing this Lenten season?

Prayer

Lord Jesus, I have often asked for your healing power in my life, not only for physical ailments but for spiritual struggles as well. Please continue to express your power in my life. Help me grow in forgiveness. Thank you for your tender mercies. Amen.

Digging Deeper

- How has the Lord heard your prayers when you've asked for healing? Have you felt sometimes that the Lord didn't answer? Whom do you know who has prayed for healing? During Lent, are you praying for divine intervention for health?
- Ezekiel 37:1–15 is the famous passage where Ezekiel sees a vision of dry bones—people who had been dead a long time—and the Lord giving them life. How do you envision God's resurrection power operating in your life and eventual death?

Tuesday

The Bronze Serpent

Numbers 21:6–9; John 3:14–15

The story of the bronze serpent always reminds me of my mom, who was so afraid of snakes that she couldn't even look at photographs or TV shows with snakes. If she had been an ancient Israelite she would have been traumatized not only by the plague of snakes but also by the solution God presents. My grandma, however, was more resilient. Living on her small farm, she killed snakes with her hoe because she didn't want them disturbing her chickens.

The bronze serpent is an odd story, related to yesterday's theme of physical and spiritual healing being interconnected. The Israelites were in the wilderness for forty years. In the first part of the forty years, we have stories of the Israelites' unhappiness and failures of faith. Exodus 17:1–7 tells the familiar story where the people protested their lack of good water. That would make me unhappy too. Through Moses, God provided for the people, but the legacy of the people's impatience remained.

When the last part of the forty-year period begins, starting at Numbers 20, the new generation is also unhappy. The story of water in Numbers 20 is similar to that of Exodus 17, and that is probably what the text is meant to convey: the younger generation worried about God's provision also. Again in Numbers 21, the younger Israelites question God's provision and complain about the food God has given them.

God is fed up and sends snakes to bite and torment the people. They are called "fiery snakes." But Moses places a bronze serpent on a pole, so that any Israelite that gazes upon the snake will be healed of the bites of the snake.

It's puzzling that God sends deadly snakes to bite the people but soon after God provides a way to be healed from the bites.

Sometimes the Scriptures perplex us, and that is part of the joy of Bible reading.

The story of the bronze serpent (alluded to in 2 Kgs. 18:4 and 1 Cor. 10:9 as well) becomes fulfilled in Jesus. The snake illustrates God's healing power. In John 3:14–15, Jesus tells Nicodemus, "And just as Moses lifted up the serpent in the wilderness, so must the Son of Man be lifted up, that whoever believes in him may have eternal life." The text continues with the famous John 3:16.

Healing was conveyed when the person who needed healing looked up at the snake. As people in Jesus' time saw Jesus' miracles but didn't understand them (they couldn't "see" in the spiritual sense), so the healing from Jesus involved the "sight" of faith. They had to look up at Jesus—who was lifted up on the cross—and trust in his love and power.

I don't want to imply that Christ only touches the lives of people who are actively seeking him. The Bible gives us stories (like the walk to Emmaus story itself, and the story of the Samaritan woman at the well) of times when Christ richly blessed people who were unaware of him, and Ephesians 3:20–21 assures us that God can do more than we can ever imagine. And these people recognize Christ. In some hidden way, they were open to the possibility of receiving him and understanding.

There have been many times in my own life when I perceived God's guidance and blessing in my life, but only in hindsight (after much fussing and anxiety). I understand the ancient Israelites who grumbled that life was difficult, without appreciating the wonders of God at hand or acknowledging the blessings of God in the past. We can be so thankful that the Lord doesn't give up on us but patiently keeps working and working and working in our lives.

Prayer

O Master, who loves humankind and all creatures, to whom all creatures look: Help me to look to you in my times of spiritual need. Nudge me when I'm not looking to you, or when I'm looking but not perceiving. Amen.

Digging Deeper

- Find a hymnal and read the service for Holy Communion (the Lord's Supper). How do you understand Communion? What connections do you see with the story of the bronze snake, Jesus, and Communion?
- Think of times you messed up (a little bit or really badly) and God gave you more chances. If you're like me, you have many such examples. What happened, and what did God do?

Wednesday

Living Water

Isaiah 12:3; Zechariah 14:8; John 4:1–42; 7:37–39

We all know the story of Jesus and the Samaritan woman at the well in John 4. I wish we knew her name.

Samaritans considered themselves descendants of the northern Israelite tribes, who were conquered by the Assyrians in 722 BCE. Their Bible was the Samaritan version of the Torah as well as some other writings, and they believed that Mount Gerizim was the holy place that God chose, rather than Jerusalem. In her conversation with Jesus, the woman referred to this difference, as well as to the well that traditionally originated from the patriarch Jacob, whom she considered her ancestor, too.

We may be tempted to fill in details of the woman's story of several marriages and present cohabitation. Let's just say she's like you and me: she has faced difficulties and disappointments in her life, and her current situation may be difficult, too. Plus, the fact that she went to the well at an inconvenient time of day suggests that she was lonely in her community. She needs a little help, or a lot. Jesus has a lot.

The story of Jesus and the woman is wonderful, the way Jesus gains her attention by even talking to her in the first place, then taking her step-by-step in a process of trust-building and understanding.

He talks about living water. The woman hears that phrase nonmetaphorically. Water is heavy to lift and carry, so she thinks of fresh, flowing water with easy, even immediate access for her thirst and other household needs. What a blessing would be fresh water for her, always at hand. Finally, he reveals himself to her, and she joyfully tells others what she's experienced.

Jesus' phrase "living water" is shortly explained, in John 7:37–39, when Jesus calls to people to believe in him so that they, too, can have this water. John writes that living water is the Spirit of

God, but the Spirit had at that time not yet been given because Jesus had not yet been glorified. The festival referred to is the feast of the tabernacles, and on the last day, the priest poured fresh water all around the altar. So Jesus is referring to a rite that was actually being done as he spoke. He is a new source of water for people seeking God.

The text says that Jesus refers to a Scripture, "Out of the believer's heart shall flow rivers of living water." This is actually not a specific Bible passage, but it echoes some beautiful passages like Isaiah 12:3, "With joy you will draw water from the wells of salvation"; Zechariah 14:8, "On that day living waters shall flow out from Jerusalem"; as well as Proverbs 18:4, Isaiah 43:19–20, Jeremiah 2:13, Ezekiel 47, and others.[2] Water is, of course, essential for life. The Bible begins and ends with images of water (Gen. 1:1–9; Rev. 22:1–3). So Jesus fulfills a general Old Testament linkage of water and life, both of which are ultimately God's gifts.

I struggle with this passage about living water. Although I am a faithful Christian (persistent if not always consistent, as our pastor says about herself), I experience times of spiritual "dryness," when I feel discouraged or "neutral" toward matters of faith. Living water seems less readily available than Jesus promised.

And yet, even in those times, when my faith is weak, I know where to turn. I turn to Christ. Just as a family member or friend loves you even when you don't love yourself very much, Christ is faithful and loving to us regardless of how we feel emotionally. Likewise the Spirit is always with us, whether we realize it or not.

How do we respond to the idea that Jesus' "living water" will take care of our thirst? How does Jesus slake your thirst? Another pastor friend put it this way: What is it about Jesus that you couldn't do without?

Prayer

Lord of the Waters, O Holy Spirit: like the Samaritan woman, I feel surprised by your love, acceptance, and promise. Like her, I feel tired from the same old chores, the same old struggles. As you did for her, help me see the blessings that make for new beginnings. Amen.

Digging Deeper

- Do you like to swim? Do you have any favorite swimming spots, past or present? Think of jumping into cool water on a hot day, and ask yourself if your faith makes you feel, in an analogous way, relieved and refreshed.
- Were there times in your life when you crossed social boundaries in a significant way? What was the situation?

Thursday
Manna and Living Bread
Exodus 16:13–21; John 6:22–40

Jesus is not just the Water of Life but also the Bread of Life. We do not live on bread alone (Deut. 8:3); God sustains us and wants to meet our physical and spiritual needs.

The only miracle of Jesus recorded in all four Gospels, other than the resurrection, is the miraculous feeding of the thousands (Matt. 14:13–21; Mark 6:30–44; Luke 9:10–17; John 6:1–14). A large crowd assembles to hear Jesus. The people are hungry. Jesus, who is filled with compassion for them, divides five loaves and two fish to feed the crowd, with plenty of food left over.

There is another miraculous feeding that this story fulfills: the story of the manna in Exodus 16. The Israelites had recently entered the wilderness, and they had immediate needs. Where would they stay? Where would they find adequate food and water? This was no excursion of a group of people hitting the road in well-stocked RVs. How many of us have similarly thought, "Maybe God won't provide for me this time, though God has provided for me before." That's my own default mode of worry.

God provided for the people across many years. Each morning, a sweet substance appeared, "it was like coriander seed, white, and the taste of it was like wafers made with honey" (Exod. 16:31). The word "manna" is Hebrew for "What is it?" which is what the Hebrews asked when they saw it. The manna sustained them throughout the wilderness time (Josh. 5:12).

Following John's telling of the story, Jesus points out to the people that God provided "bread from heaven" in order to feed and sustain God's people. Jesus then draws a comparison between that bread, which though of miraculous origin was only temporarily sustaining, whereas Jesus himself is the true bread of life. Though we'll die physically, Jesus the bread sustains us spiritually

64

and provides us with life with God that will never end (John 6:47–51).

But Jesus' words sounded repellant. He spoke of the consumption of his flesh and blood. Jewish kosher laws forbid the consumption of any blood, and eating human flesh is taboo in nearly all cultures. Understood in hindsight, Jesus spoke of his crucified body and shed blood distributed among believers in the Eucharistic elements, through which God's sacramental grace comes to us.

In our John passage, Jesus' use of the phrase "I am" is not just the component of a grammatically correct sentence. It harkens back to the salvation of the people from Egyptian slavery, first promised to Moses:

> God said to Moses, "I AM WHO I AM." He said further, "Thus you shall say to the Israelites, 'I AM has sent me to you.'" God also said to Moses, "Thus you shall say to the Israelites, 'The LORD, the God of your ancestors, the God of Abraham, the God of Isaac, and the God of Jacob, has sent me to you.'" (Exod. 3:13–15)

This, too, seemed blasphemous to Jesus' hearers: Jesus has identity of being and purpose with the God of their heritage. Neither a king nor a prophet would claim such a thing. It wasn't until the resurrection that Jesus' relationship with God became clearer to many. Thus, the Emmaus friends did not recognize the Lord, nor understand who he really was, until he broke bread with them in a sacramental way.

The manna was a supernaturally provided kind of bread that, although spiritual in origin, sustained the physical lives of the Israelites during their years in the wilderness. Jesus speaks of himself as a supernatural bread of life that sustains us spiritually—and, indeed, sustains our lives now, re-creates us and makes us righteous (2 Cor. 5:21), and carries us into life beyond the grave.

Prayer
Holy Bread of Life: I feel burdened by sins and worries, but I look to you for help. Open my heart to eucharistic grace. Amen.

Digging Deeper
- What is your favorite food? If you were facing execution, what would you request at your last meal?
- In Matthew 5:6, Jesus blesses those who hunger and thirst for righteousness. What do you think that means?

Friday

The Poor and Needy

Jeremiah 22:16; Luke 6:20

Jesus meets our spiritual needs as well as the needs of our physical bodies. But sometimes we forget that Jesus addresses people's social and economic well-being as well.

This, too, is a strong Old Testament theme that Jesus can be affirmed to fulfill: God's concern for the poor and the needy. If Jesus discussed this aspect of the Scriptures on the walk to Emmaus, he might have used quite a bit of time and mileage! In Jeremiah 22:16, God speaks approvingly of King Josiah, one of the few righteous Old Testament kings. Josiah addressed the needs of the poor, and God declared that *this is the way to know God.*

The Scriptures are full of references to God's concern for the poor: God cares for the poor (Deut. 10:17–18; Ps. 10:17–18; 12:5; 14:6; and others). Those who help the poor are happy and commended (for example, Prov. 14:21; 28:27), while those who oppress the poor are condemned (Deut. 27:19; Prov. 17:5; Isa. 10:1–4). Worship is only meaningful when combined with justice (Isa. 2:3–4; Mic. 4:1–8). The Torah contains provisions to help people have economic justice and well-being, such as collateral-free loans, care for resident aliens and orphans, debt cancellations, generosity, and so on (for example: Lev. 25:35–37; Deut. 15:1–18; Deut. 24:10–22). According to one Jewish author, the commands to give to the poor are so important that ancient rabbis believed these commands are equal to all the other commandments together.[3] The motive of this ethic is that the Lord rescued the people from their Egyptian slavery, so they must never forget to help rescue others in need.[4]

So many Bible verses call attention to the poor and needy. Passages like Hosea 6:6 (referred to in Matt. 9:13 that we read earlier this week) as well as Jeremiah 9:24 also remind us that God is a God of loving-kindness, justice, and righteousness—and that these have social implications.[5] Remember Luke 4:16–19, wherein Jesus announces good news to the poor. Reread Mary's Magnificat in Luke 1:46–55 and the way she praises God for God's care of the needy. Luke's Gospel emphasizes care for the poor, as in the Beatitudes: Matthew quotes Jesus as saying, "Blessed are the poor in spirit," but Luke quotes him as saying, "Blessed are the poor" (Luke 6:20).

Many other Bible passages apply to this theme: Matthew 25:31–46 and James 2:1–17, for instance. Galatians 2:9–10 indicates strong agreement between Peter, James, John, and Paul—noted for their disagreements on other things—on the matter of helping the poor. Matthew 6:24 stipulates that we can't serve two masters, and 1 Timothy 6:9–10, 17–19 warns that the desire for riches is a trap. The famous "render unto Caesar" saying of Mark 12:17 indicates that God is greater than even the strong powers of our society: the government and the economy. But that great God is the same Lord who calls us to love and care for the poor, however we decide and feel led to reach out and befriend those less fortunate.

One of the famous examples of Jesus' attitude is the rich young ruler (Luke 18:18–23). Many times I've read that story as a call to give away all one's money and become indigent for the Lord, a choice that obviously most people do not choose. But I missed a crucial point: *the man had no compassion for the poor.* Jesus gave him a specific thing to do with his money: help the poor. The man exhibited no sadness toward the poor that could make Jesus' command seem like a meaningful opportunity.

Too many Christians are prone to feel disdainful toward the poor. God takes the side of those in economic distress. Jesus' teachings are consistent with the Old Testament. That slogan, "What Would Jesus Do?" was again popular several years ago. I believe that loving those in need, in whatever way you can, is among the top answers to that question.

Prayer

Dear Lord: "Those who mock the poor insult their Maker" (Prov. 17:5), and I confess that has been me, many times. I have viewed my struggling neighbor as someone who is lazy and no good. Open my heart with your compassion and, in turn, your compassion can flow from me to those who look for economic and social well-being. Amen.

Digging Deeper
Visit a food pantry or other ministry that helps those in poverty. Read up on the subjects of poverty, hunger, and health.

Saturday

Lord of the Sabbath

Exodus 20:8–11; 31:12–17; Deuteronomy 5:12–15;
Matthew 12:1–8

One more lesson on the theme of Jesus and our well-being.
For Jews, Sabbath (Friday sundown till Saturday sundown) is a matter of joy and well-being (Isa. 58:13). The day is a beautiful, hallowed gift from God, not a day of repentance but of eating, worship, and prayers, consciousness of God's blessings, rest from work, and time with family. The ancient scriptural tradition that includes Genesis chapter 1, wherein God rests on the seventh day, is the same tradition that includes Exodus 31, where the Sabbath is part of God's "perpetual covenant" with his people (Exod. 31:16–17). This is also the section that includes the authorization of the tabernacle. Thus, God not only establishes that physical space but also a temporal "place" where Israel can worship God. Of course, the Sabbath is also the subject of the Fourth Commandment (Exod. 20:8–11, Deut. 5:12–15).[6]

For Jews, human need comes first. As a Holocaust survivor once explained to me, if you have a choice to go to services or to take someone to the hospital, that duty to help another person supersedes formal acts of worship. Jesus' attitude about the Sabbath is much like the prevailing Jewish attitude. Many of the people in my life whom I admire most are Jewish friends and colleagues who strive to make people's lives better every day.

So what, then, was the situation with Jesus and the Sabbath during that time period? As Huston Smith writes, "It was the Pharisees that Jesus stood closest to, for the difference between them was one of emphasis only. The Pharisees stressed Yahweh's holiness, while Jesus stressed Yahweh's compassion, but the Pharisees would have been the first to insist that Yahweh was also compassionate, and Jesus that Yahweh was holy."[7] But Jesus believed that the laws and rules to ensure people's holiness created a social structure that excluded people from God's compassion.[8]

In the story from Matthew 12, Jesus refers to an incident in David's life, when he ate the "bread of the presence" that sat upon the gold table in the tabernacle. This bread was baked and set out every Sabbath, and only Aaron and his sons would eat the bread (Exod. 25:30; Lev. 24:8–9; Heb. 9:1–2). But David was hungry and ate the bread when he was fleeing Saul (1 Sam. 21:1–6; Matt. 12:1–8; Mark 2:25–27, and Luke 6:3–5). Although David's actions were improper, he was in need, and Jesus used this example to teach about human need.

But like the healing miracle in John 5 (which also happened on the Sabbath), Jesus also taught about his own identity. "The Son of Man is lord of the sabbath," he says in Matthew 12:8. In John's Gospel, Jesus more explicitly calls God his Father, "thereby making himself equal to God" (John 5:18).

That is a crucial takeaway from Jesus' teachings about the Sabbath. The author of Hebrews likens the rest (that is, the peace and blessing) of the Sabbath with the peace and blessing of the promised land, and then Hebrews likens both Sabbath and land to Christ's salvation, our eternal life (Heb. 4:1–13). So the blessings of Sabbath become understood through the peace and life of Jesus. Notice the location of the famous passage where Jesus bids his followers to unload their burdens and find rest in him; it's immediately prior to our Matthew passage (Matt. 11:28–30).

Christ is Lord of the Sabbath because he is also Lord of our whole lives, bringing about peace and blessing and renewal to us through the power of the Holy Spirit. Indeed, he is the Life that renews and sustains us and will carry us to heaven: our ultimate Sabbath rest.

Prayer

Dear Lord, guide me in your will, not only in the things I do and accomplish but in the way I cease my labors and look to you for rest. Help me be renewed; help me seek renewal; help me make good choices in how I structure my life. Amen.

Digging Deeper

- During the remainder of Lent, if you do not already do so, make a commitment to spend Saturday or Sunday (or some other available day) as a Sabbath time when you cease your work, relax, and honor God.
- If you're off work on weekends, what do you typically like to do on those days? What would be your ideal weekend?

Fourth Sunday Reflection

We just saw that creation and Sabbath are biblically related. Are you a person who gets spiritual inspiration and a sense of well-being through walking in nature? In turn, do you think of Jesus Christ when you are outdoors?

The Psalms praise God as the author of life. Read Psalms 19 and 104; God provides for all the creatures of the earth, establishes the natural processes of the earth, and creates the geological forms. All things praise God, not in human song and speech, but in the ways that they can (Ps. 19:1–4). Of course, Genesis 1 and 2 narrate the origin and goodness of all things.

That favorite hymn, "How Great Thou Art," links the wonders of the natural world with the glories of Jesus Christ. One of my favorite Bible passages is from Colossians 1:15–20, where Christ is described as

> the image of the invisible God, the firstborn of all creation;
> for in him all things in heaven and on earth were created,
> things visible and invisible, whether thrones or dominions
> or rulers or powers—all things have been created through
> him and for him. He himself is before all things, and in him
> all things hold together. (vv.16–17)

The passage goes on to praise Christ as head of the church and the "firstborn from the dead," and the power of reconciliation and redemption that unites us with God and one another.

But in Christ we are "new creations." As we are given the gift of physical life as God's creatures, we are given the gift of divine life as new creatures in God's eternal kingdom. That gift of divine life includes the spiritual renewal that is analogous to the natural process. Believers in Christ are made new (2 Cor. 4:16–18). The church, in turn, is part of the new creation (2 Cor. 5:17), the site of our new life (Col. 3:9–15). Analogous to the growth we experience in physical life, we are called to spiritual growth that benefits one another (Eph. 4:11–16).[9]

This week we looked at the Lord's concern for our well-being. The Lord's concern for us is part of our overall relationship to God: the peace, balance, health, and restoration that God promises.

Prayer

Lord God, maker of heaven and earth, help me to have greater awareness of your presence in my life and in the lives of others. We thank you for the beauty of your creation and your love that sustains the cosmos. Fill me with the kindness and compassion you show to all beings. Amen.

Digging Deeper

Do you think you are any different because you're a Christian? How do you think your life would be different if you were not? What kind of Christian would you still like to be?

Monday

The Exodus

Exodus 12:37–14:31

Across the two Testaments, the Bible is the story of one God and one salvation. As we continue our Lenten journey through the Scriptures, let's look at six great, interrelated themes of salvation in the Old Testament and see how they continue in the life and work of Jesus.

If someone asked you what the Bible is about, what would you say?

In the first section of the Bible, the Torah, we read a beautiful story of God's salvation that includes the life of Moses, the rescue of the Israelites from Egyptian slavery, the splitting of the sea, the establishment of the covenant in the wilderness, the Israelites' experiences in the wilderness, and finally their entry into the promised land under Joshua's leadership.

Think of this great story as a "model" of God's wonderful salvation. The story, in whole or in part, permeates the whole Bible.

Where do we get the idea of God as a savior, as a rescuer, as a covenant-maker? Right here.

We have already thought about the escape of Jesus and his parents to Egypt. Jesus' forty days in the wilderness harkens back to the Israelites' forty years in the wilderness. We saw the parallel of the wilderness manna and Jesus' bread of life.

As we'll discuss when we get to Maundy Thursday, the Passover miracle (which involved lambs' blood) was a salvation from death, and the blood of Jesus (the Lamb of God) saves us from the power of death. The first Lord's Supper was likely a Passover meal, and our Eucharist (Lord's Supper) has elements of Passover. So the escape from Egypt has a fulfillment in our escape (salvation) from sin and death.

Other examples include Jesus' very name ("Yeshua," or Joshua, which means "the Lord saves"), and the parallel between Moses and the mountain and Jesus' Sermon on the Mount (Matt. 5–7). When Mary praises God in the Magnificat (Luke 1:46–55), she praises a God who is mindful of the needs of his people.

In the New Testament letters, Paul uses Exodus imagery in describing the Christian life. When you have time, read 1 Corinthians 5:7; 10:1–5 and 2 Corinthians 3:4–18.[1] In Romans, Paul retells the exodus story as a story of moving from sin and death (analogous to Egyptian slavery) to freedom in Christ and the inheritance, not of the promised land this time but of the blessings of Christ. Jesus' rescue (salvation) from the slavery of sin is consistent with God's great acts rescuing the Israelites from Egyptian slavery. Paul draws from the longtime hope of the Old Testament prophets who looked to God to continue working on behalf of God's people in ways consistent with the liberation from Egypt.[2]

Even the final liberation depicted in Revelation can be considered a fulfillment of the exodus. As one writer puts it, "The first triumphant Exodus has prefigured the second and we are to look ahead to its fulfillment in God's victory at the end of time."[3]

Christians also depend upon the God of the rescued Israelites for . . . well, everything concerning our faith. Jesus and the other New Testament figures aren't just extra people tacked onto the Hebrew Scriptures but the people God created and, hundreds of years before, rescued under Moses' leadership. We Gentiles are part of this heritage through God's kindness and mercy (Rom. 9:25; 11:17–22).

Prayer

Dear Lord, you blessed your people Israel and showed to us that you are a righteous Lord. In our own ways, we need freedom from different kinds of oppression. Reach out to us and lead us during these days. Amen.

Digging Deeper

Do you have a favorite movie about the exodus? The 1956 movie *The Ten Commandments* is perhaps the most famous. Do you have a favorite part of that whole story?

Tuesday

Covenant

Exodus 34:1–28; Jeremiah 31:31–34

Not long after splitting the sea, God establishes an everlasting agreement with God's people that involves the giving of laws in Exodus 20–23, the making of the covenant in 24:1–8, and its renewal in 34:10–28. Hard as it may be to picture, the splitting of the sea was a prelude to God's covenant rather than the covenant being an important postlude to God's ostentatious miracle.

Covenant is a formal agreement between God and people. The word derives from the Latin *con venire*, translated as "coming together."[4] In the original languages of the Bible, the word is used over 300 times in both Testaments[5] (and "testament" is just an old English word for "covenant"). Throughout history, beginning with Abraham, circumcision has been the sign of the Hebrew covenant.

There are several covenants in the Bible: between God and Noah, Abraham, Moses, the Priests, David, and the new covenant, of which Jeremiah writes in this beautiful passage:

The days are surely coming, says the LORD, when I will make a new covenant with the house of Israel and the house of Judah. It will not be like the covenant that I made with their ancestors when I took them by the hand to bring them out of the land of Egypt—a covenant that they broke, though I was their husband, says the LORD. But this is the covenant that I will make with the house of Israel after those days, says the LORD: I will put my law within them, and I will write it on their hearts; and I will be their God, and they shall be my people. No longer shall they teach one another, or say to each other, "Know the LORD," for they shall all know me, from the least of them to the greatest, says the LORD; for I

will forgive their iniquity, and remember their sin no more.
(Jeremiah 31:31–34)

This passage is the source of the phrase "New Testament"
("New Covenant") which is found several times in the Scriptures
(Luke 22:20; 1 Cor. 11:25; Heb. 8:6–13; and others). As we will
see, Jesus established the new covenant at the Last Supper.

Have you thought of your life as one of covenant? Any time we
talk about following the Ten Commandments, we are stating that
we are living under a covenant with God and are seeking to be
obedient. Every time we take Communion in church, we affirm
that we are in covenant with God. Any time we feel happy that
we're in a relationship with God, we say that we're in covenant
with God—that God has promised certain things to us and that
God is true.

God establishes covenant out of love, but it is not a shallow,
"nice" love. As Walter Brueggemann writes, "The ground of the
new covenant is rigorous demand. The covenant requires that
Israel undertake complete loyalty to God in a social context where
attractive alternatives exist."[6] God wants people to be devoted to
God, to be holy, and to spurn things that would keep us from
God or distract us from God. But that is so difficult, because
nearly anything can distract us from our relationship with God.

But God is always faithful, as expressed in a moving way elsewhere in Jeremiah:

> Thus says the LORD: If any of you could break my covenant
> with the day and my covenant with the night, so that day
> and night would not come at their appointed time, only then
> could my covenant with my servant David be broken, so that
> he would not have a son to reign on his throne. (Jeremiah
> 33:20–21)

Prayer

Holy Light, our refuge and help: many things distract us from
our relationship with you. We ask your forgiveness for our sin

and weakness, and we rejoice in your constant love. Keep us on the straight path of covenant fidelity. Amen.

Digging Deeper

If one wanted to be completely devoted to God, one might join a religious order of some sort. But most of us try to be devoted to God while going about our everyday lives. What distracts you from your own faithfulness to God? What enhances and strengthens it?

Wednesday
The Law
Psalm 119:33–40; Matthew 5:17–20

Covenant is the agreement and law is the content of the covenant for God's people. Torah, another name for the Bible's first five books, means law or instruction. The books contain legal material and also include that great story from creation to the death of Moses.

The number of laws in the Torah is traditionally numbered at 613. About 300 are still observed by some Jews today. Some of the laws cannot be followed in modern times; for instance, the laws concerning the priesthood and Temple cannot be followed because those no longer exist. Jews debate whether the agricultural laws apply only to the land of Israel or also other places. Many other laws can certainly be followed in one's daily life. Jews among different branches of Judaism differ in their approach to observance of the laws but all the laws are considered a precious gift from God and are read, eagerly studied, and taught for ethical instruction, for their levels of meaning, and for devotion.[7]

Matthew recorded Jesus' words in the Sermon on the Mount:

> "Do not think that I have come to abolish the law or the prophets; I have come not to abolish but to fulfill. For truly I tell you, until heaven and earth pass away, not one letter, not one stroke of a letter, will pass from the law until all is accomplished." (Matt. 5:17–18)

But when Gentiles first started to join the Christian fellowship (which was still considered Jewish), the question was raised: Do they have to keep the Jewish law and covenant? For instance, did the males have to be circumcised as the sign of the covenant, as Genesis 17:10–14 commanded?

The answer was no. The first church council authorized a

few basic requirements for Gentiles that also were important in Torah observance (Acts 15:1–35, especially verses 19–21). The Apostle Paul argued that since Gentile Christians had been given the gift of God's Spirit, they were clearly accepted and loved by God. Therefore, Paul said, they did not also have to convert to Judaism, and the men did not have to undergo circumcision (Gal. 3:2). Gentiles also follow the great commandments of love, which are of course part of the law and indeed key verses for the whole law!

After Paul had his experience meeting the risen Christ, he understood that Jesus' law-keeping was a fulfillment of righteousness—as we've seen other actions of Jesus in that regard. In Paul's understanding, the law defined what is sin: God wants us to do these things but also not to do other things (Rom. 7:7–13). But it is in our nature to stray from sound rules and laws (Rom. 7:14–25). Paul saw no way around his sinful nature unless God provides more help.

Paul understood Jesus to be that help. Jesus kept the Law, but because of Jesus' death and resurrection, God has declared us righteous (sinners who have been rescued by God) apart from our observance of the Law. Jesus' death and resurrection is what was "accomplished" in Jesus' words that we read above. If we look to Jesus, God saves (justifies) us through our faith, not by anything we "bring to the table," even in our best obedience to God.

Paul stayed within the Torah but went earlier into the Torah, before Moses, to prove his point. Abraham had faith in God and God declared Abraham a righteous person. But Abraham lived hundreds of years before Moses and the Law. Abraham is an illustration of how God blesses and saves us before we're able to respond to and keep any law—just because of faith alone.

The other "accomplishment" to which Jesus refers is the giving of the Holy Spirit. Read Ephesians 2:13–22, where the author writes about that idea of new creation—in this case, a new humanity united in Christ, with no barriers between Jew and Gentile (or any other boundaries).

To put it another way, Jesus opens up the "new covenant" with believers, so that the law is written "on their hearts" (Jer.

31:33–34; also Deut. 10:16; 30:6), and the law is followed through the Spirit and through love. Thus, as Jesus says, the law is never abolished.

Prayer

Divine Light for all our ways, we praise you and thank you. We want to please you. But we also want to go our own way. Praise to you that our waywardness and sin never separate us from you. Continue to be with us and with our friends and families during this season and beyond. Amen.

Digging Deeper

- Memorize Psalm 119:105: "Your word is a lamp to my feet and a light to my path."
- Consider a Bible study of Romans or Galatians. Learn more about how Paul preaches Christ as a way we are saved by faith and grace alone.

Thursday

The Law and the Prophets

Psalm 97:1–2; Daniel 7:9–10; Mark 9:2–13

The story of Jesus' transfiguration is found in Matthew 17:1–8, Mark 9:2–8, and Luke 9:28–36. Jesus took Peter, James, and John to the top of an unnamed mountain, likely Mount Tabor (Josh. 19:22 and Judg. 4:6). There, Jesus transfigured (the Greek word is *metamorphoō*). "[H]is clothes became dazzling white, such as no one on earth could bleach them" (Mark 9:3: think of our first-week reflection on Malachi, fuller's soap, and holiness). Moses and Elijah appeared and talked to Jesus. Peter, always trying his best, did not know what to say but at least offered them hospitality. A voice came from the cloud, "This is my Son, the Beloved; listen to him!" (Mark 9:7). With that, the event ended.

There are several significant things about this event. One is certainly the appearance of Jesus in his glorified nature. His normal appearance was ordinary, and even after he rose from death, he was not immediately recognized—certainly not shining with the dazzling glory of the transfiguration. The story forms an "arc" back to Jesus' baptism, when the Holy Spirit descended as a dove and the voice of God similarly announced Jesus' relationship to God (Matt. 3:17; Mark 1:11; Luke 1:22). The event also connects to the upcoming future, the ascension, when Jesus would rise and thus validate his promises and inaugurate God's new kingdom. How satisfying when we see the Bible's interconnections.

As in many religious traditions, natural objects like rivers, trees, and mountains are important in different Bible passages. We associate Moses with Mount Sinai and also with Mount Nebo, where he looked across to the promised land and was buried. Moses, in fact, literally glowed with his proximity to God's presence on Sinai (Exod. 34:29–35).[8] We also associate Elijah with Mount Horeb, where he had an experience of the Lord's instruction (1 Kgs. 19:11–18).

The presence of Moses and Elijah are significant to show how Jesus fulfills Scripture. The phrase "the Law and the Prophets" is frequently found in the Gospels, not only to refer to the Old Testament but as a euphemism for God's promises. By appearing alongside Jesus, Moses and Elijah signify the continuity of the law and the prophets with Jesus, who continues and fulfills God's promises in the new covenant.

Moses, of course, was the great leader and law-giver who led the people from Egypt. Elijah was not a "writing prophet," that is, we have stories about him in 1 and 2 Kings but no Bible books of his authorship; nevertheless he is considered one of the greatest prophets, one who miraculously ascended to heaven (2 Kgs. 2:11–12). He is still referred to in the services of the Sabbath and Passover.

We thought about the prophets in an earlier lesson. In continuity with the Law and the Prophets, the New Testament writings make many connections to the prophets, several of which we explore in this book. Anyone hoping to gain deeper knowledge of the Bible can spend fulfilling time tracing the prophetic roots of the New Testament.

We can also draw connections with that word *metamorphoō*, which as you could guess means to change form. When I was in divinity school, I was pleased to learn that the word was the same as the one in Romans 12:2, "Do not be conformed to this world, but be transformed by the renewing of your minds, so that you may discern what is the will of God—what is good and acceptable and perfect." The good news is that our own transformation is not our own doing, although our choices and our obedience enter into the process. The glory and holiness of Jesus is a power that transforms us over time. Even for us now, that can be frightening.

Prayer

El Shaddai, enthroned between the cherubim, we, too, tremble at your majesty, and our words fail us. But when words fail you intervene with "sighs too deep for words." The glory of Christ on the mountain lightens our darkness with the power that draws us to you in love and redeems us for all time and eternity. Amen.

Digging Deeper

- Have you ever had a "mountaintop experience," that is, an especially uplifting experience? It could be literally an experience of a high place, or an event that was especially moving and life-changing. What happened? How did it affect your life? What was the aftermath? (Note that aftermaths can be disappointing: Moses' "mountaintop experience" was followed by the incident of the golden calf.)
- How do you think you have changed over the years as a result of your belief in the Lord?

Friday

Priesthood

Exodus 29:1–9; Leviticus 16; Hebrews 4:14–5:10

God loves us even at our absolute worst and never gives up on us. This faithfulness of God's is expressed in different ways. Today and tomorrow, I want to think about Jesus' relationship to the ancient Israelite priesthood and sacrificial system. These are other aspects of covenant, law, and salvation.

If you're like me, you sometimes find yourself in situations where you want, even long for, someone to take your side. You want someone to stand up for you. Think of any movie or story where the main character is in trouble and looks to another character, someone stronger or better positioned, for help.

As we thought about on the second Wednesday lesson, God demands a holy people. In the biblical history, the priests were important aspects of that holiness. Think of priests as those men who took the side of sinners. On the Day of Atonement, the high priest entered the holiest place of the Temple and stood in the special location of God's holy presence. He sprinkled blood on the cover of the ark of the covenant so that the people's sins were "covered." On other days, the priests made sacrifices for the people, and also for themselves, since they too were sinful and mortal. These were the blessed ways that God stipulated for holy worship at that time.

We find much information about the priests in Exodus 28–29 and Leviticus 8–10, and about different kinds of sacrifices in Leviticus 1–7. The priestly benediction, which we use in our churches, is found in Numbers 6:24–25. Aaron (Moses' brother) and his sons are consecrated to an eternal priesthood, and the Aaronic priests are authorized to perform sacrificial and other rites, while Levites were responsible for maintenance of the tabernacle (e.g. Num. 1:47–54).[9]

Israel's sacrifices were strongly connected to having a right heart and a right motive, not a notion that God required nourishment or placation. The rituals were connected to true righteousness, morality, service to others, and loyalty to God. Otherwise the rituals meant nothing (Amos 5:21–24; Ps. 51:16–19; compare that idea with the famous 1 Cor. 13:1–7).

With the destruction of the Temple in 70 CE, Jewish sacrifices came to an end and have never been revived. In keeping with that biblical theme of a right heart and care for others, Jews have, in many ways, replaced sacrifices with acts of charity and service.

Early Christian thinkers like Paul and the author of Hebrews articulated a problem with the sacrifices of Bible times: sacrifices had to be done over and over again. As long as people sinned (which is forever), sacrifices would be necessary. By analogy, we might say that people need to bathe as long as they perspire and get dirty. In kind with the impermanence of sacrifices, there was no single "eternal high priest," any more than there was an eternal human king. Generation after generation, there were new priests.

The author of the book of Hebrews calls Jesus our perfect high priest. Jesus did not have to make sacrifices for himself because he was already holy, "a Son . . . perfect forever" (Heb. 7:28). Jesus was mortal, but in his resurrection he conquered death. Thus he is our high priest forever.

Jesus is also tenderhearted, merciful, and compassionate. One of my favorite Bible passages is Hebrews 4:15–16:

> For we do not have a high priest who is unable to sympathize with our weaknesses, but we have one who in every respect has been tested as we are, yet without sin. Let us therefore approach the throne of grace with boldness, so that we may receive mercy and find grace to help in time of need.

As a temple priest was conscious of human weakness and sin because of the necessity of sacrificing for himself, Jesus the eternal priest understands our sin and weakness—in an omnipotent way—and takes our side.

We are daily, lifelong beneficiaries of Jesus' compassionate priestly work.

Prayer

Priest Jesus, what a wonderful thought that you know me better than I know myself and, in spite of all my known and hidden sin and weakness, you take my side. You take my sins and mistakes, cover them, and transform them for good. Thank you! Bless my church and the churches of my community. Amen.

Digging Deeper

- Drawing on Old Testament theology of the Temple and priesthood, Paul teaches that we are holy because we have the Holy Spirit within (for instance, 1 Cor. 3:17). Do you ever think of yourself as holy? God calls his people "a priestly kingdom and a holy nation" (Exod. 19:6, et al.). Think about how we are holy in relationship to God, and how that translates into our own lives.

- Jesus was not a member of the tribe of Levi, that is, the priestly tribe, but rather that of Judah, David's tribe. But the book of Hebrews connects Jesus to another priest of God, Melchizedek (Gen. 14:17–24), as another kind of priestly order that God has blessed (Ps. 110:4). Read Hebrews 5:5–10 and 6:19–7:19 and learn how Jesus is described as a "better priest" by being connected to Melchizedek. We'll return to this man in our Easter lesson.

Saturday

Sacrifices

Leviticus 1, 3, 4; Romans 3:21–26; Hebrews 7:26–28; 9:11–28

When I was a child I learned this old hymn:

> Are you washed in the blood,
> In the soul-cleansing blood of the Lamb?
> Are your garments spotless? Are they white as snow?
> Are you washed in the blood of the Lamb?"

I also learned the hymn, "It is Well with My Soul."

> My sin—oh, the bliss of this glorious thought!—
> My sin, not in part but the whole,
> Is nailed to the cross, and I bear it no more,
> Praise the Lord, praise the Lord, O my soul!"

Likely you know the word "atonement," which Paul uses in our lesson from Romans. It means reparation or a satisfaction for a wrong, or reconciliation after a wrong. In religion, the word signifies reconciliation between God and humans. Paul uses the phrase, "a sacrifice of atonement by [Christ's] blood" (Rom. 3:25).

Atonement is a widely interpreted aspect of Christian belief. One can look at Jesus' death as a payment for the enormity of human sin, so that all our own sins are "nailed to the cross." Jesus took the punishment we deserved. Another way is reflected in old-time hymns: that the blood "washes" our sins away. Other theologians argue that Jesus's death and resurrection was a battle over the power of Satan, sin, and death. A similar view is that Jesus' resurrection is a victory over the worldly powers that killed him, and thus it establishes God's authority over all powers. One can also see Jesus' death as God's loving identification with the terrible suffering in the world. Similarly, his death can be understood as an example of exemplary love, since Jesus entered that suffering and asked forgiveness for the people involved.

In biblical times, blood was considered the life force, which of course it is, but also it was understood to convey spiritual power. God is the creator of life, and the essence of life's sacredness is blood. Observant Jews refrain from consuming blood and from eating meat from which the blood hasn't been carefully removed.

The different types of sacrifices are described in Leviticus 1–7. In an animal sacrifice, the creature gave its life as a substitute for the life of the sinner offering the sacrifice. The slain animal could not be an expendable one from among your livestock. As the sacrifice cost the animal everything, its death also had to cost you something: it was a valuable animal that could have been lucrative for you. Paul's idea of making ourselves "a living sacrifice" (Rom. 12:1) communicates the personal costliness and personal commitment of sacrifices. Think of the poor widow in Luke 21:1–4; "sacrifice" meant for her not just the physical death of a bird or animal but "sacrifice" in the sense of risky, personal expense.

In yesterday's lesson, we thought about how Jesus is the perfect priest. But he is also the perfect sacrifice. He did not die on an altar, but he gave himself freely to death in a way that involved loss of his blood. Like a sacrificial animal, his gift to God cost him everything. In the language of the book of Hebrews, Christ entered the holy place as high priest but offered his own blood to cover our sins. Because he was the Son of God, his blood has infinite power for everyone, not simply the power of an altar sacrifice in a particular time. The blood of the Incarnate God is the power of life itself. Thus (the author of Hebrews continues), Jesus' sacrifice does not need to be repeated over and over again, nor was it aimed at the particular sins of particular individuals. It was done once for the sins of everyone who believe. And like the words of the hymn, his blood covers our sin "not in part, but the whole."

When we studied "covenant" earlier this week, we thought about how God's love is demanding and costly. In Jesus, we see how much "investment" God made to love us. What a comforting thought, that when we're at our worst in our deepest hearts, we are objects of God's love, active on our behalf.

Prayer

Lamb of God, you take away the sins of the world. You have died on our behalf so that we are free to love God without reservation. Help us allow those truths to "sink in" and become meaningful to us this season. Amen.

Digging Deeper

- Consult a Bible dictionary and read more about biblical sacrifices and about the atonement.
- The idea of "nonviolent atonement" has gained currency in theological discussions over the past several years. Recognizing the violence perpetrated against people in contemporary society (like battered spouses, American slaves, and many others), the idea is to move beyond a theology where God demands violence against his passively obedient Son to a theology where Jesus' death is the occasion for him to defeat the power of Satan, to display transformative love, and to actively take our side in the human condition. How would you explain the atonement to someone asking you about it?

Fifth Sunday Reflection

The prophet Habakkuk writes, "the righteous live by their faith" (Hab. 2:4).

The word translated "faith" is *emuna*, which means steadfastness, trustworthiness, and fidelity.[10]

Expressed this way, God has "faith," too. That is, God can be counted on. God is trustworthy and is faithful to the covenant.

The New Testament applies this verse to Christian experience. It is quoted in Romans 1:17; Galatians 3:11; and Hebrews 10:38. In these passages, "faith" can mean ascent to the declaration that Jesus is God's Son. Paul wants to demonstrate that anyone is saved (lives) if she has faith in Christ, apart from obedience to the Jewish law (which Gentiles weren't required to adopt).

But in these passages, "faith" can also have the deeper meaning: We believe, because God has been faithful and trustworthy, and the life and actions of Jesus show that God continues to be faithful. Affirming and trusting the faithfulness of God across the centuries is to live.

Our Scriptures this week show how the good news of Jesus follows upon the wonderful things that God has done in the past, including creation itself. We say that "God does not change," but that doesn't mean that God is predictable. Amazed and energized by their experience of Jesus, the early Christians went through the Bible and made connections among God's wonderful works and showed how they related to Jesus Christ. They saw how creation (including human beings' responsible reliance upon birds and animals and grain) related to covenant (where things of creation could have use in atonement ceremonies), and how aspects of the covenant (holiness, priesthood, and sacrifice) related to Christ.

Perhaps the early Christians' excitement upon discovering the constancy of God's love—a love that spans the biblical centuries and beyond—is something we can "catch" as we study the Scriptures with Christ during this Lenten season.

Prayer
Holy Trinity, Righteous Lord: thank you for your faithfulness across the centuries and millennia. Help me thereby to know that my problems are within a tiny portion of your providence throughout time and space. Amen.

Digging Deeper
How would you assess your own faith? Has your faith nearly vanished? Is it strong? If you're like me, the quality of your faith has been different at different times.

Monday

Noah's Ark

Genesis 6:9–9:29; Luke 17:22–32; 1 Peter 3:20

We have seen Jesus' relationship to several biblical figures, such as Moses and Elijah and others. This week, let's think about a few more Old Testament figures and images Jesus might have connected to himself as he walked to Emmaus.

Springtime has finally arrived, and the plants and trees look pretty outside. Dogwoods are in bloom. Throughout the Bible, trees and wood are connected with life and salvation, both in the sense of being essential to physical life as well as being connected to spiritual realities. We think of the Tree of Life and the Tree of the Knowledge of Good and Evil in Eden, the cypress wood that formed Noah's ark, the acacia wood used for the tabernacle and its various components (Ex. 27:1–8, 30:1–6, and others), the Lebanon cedar and other woods of Solomon's Temple (1 Kgs. 5–7, 2 Chr. 2–4), the wood of Christ's manger, the cross (the "tree" on which Christ took our curse: Deut. 21:22–23; Gal. 3:3), and finally (framing the entire Bible with a tree) the restored Tree of Life, Revelation 22:2.

Today, we think of that big wooden boat and the man who constructed it.

As a child, I learned about Noah's faith, and that was the primary lesson of the story. The animals give the story appeal; children's toys and cartoons feature the ark and its animal passengers. The story is terrible if you remove the childhood associations.

95

It's a story about the judgment of God and the loss of life. The flood did nothing to make people better: humankind starts over, but a couple chapters later, people hope to build a tower to the heavens, a new sign of rebellion (Gen. 11:1–9). But in the midst of generations of human unrighteousness, Noah believed in the promise of God and endured with his family through the ordeal.

In Isaiah 54:9, the waters of Noah become a symbol of God's promise not to be angry with his people forever. Even more, the waters saved Noah and his family from God's wrath. Now the waters of baptism also represent God's salvation through Christ's love (1 Pet. 3:20). At Christ's own baptism, the Holy Spirit appeared as a dove, the same peaceful creature that brought Noah assurance of God's salvation (Gen. 8:11).

Noah's faith is also an example of readiness, which is a key connection with the New Testament. In his parables and other teachings, Jesus warns about the coming of the Son of Man; you don't want to be caught unprepared when the Son of Man comes, for in the days of Noah only he and his family were ready (Matt. 24:32–42; Luke 17:22–32).

Jesus discouraged speculation about the timetable of the end times (Mark 13:32), but people of the New Testament era looked to his imminent, sudden return (Mark 13:36). Thus, writers like Paul encouraged people to stay alert (1 Cor. 16:13; 1 Thess. 5:1–11), though we should not neglect our daily responsibilities (2 Thess. 3:6–13). Christ "will appear a second time, not to deal with sin, but to save those who are eagerly waiting for him" (Heb. 9:28). At that time he'll be king over all earth and heaven (Rev. 11:15), will completely destroy the power of death (1 Cor. 15:25, 26), will bring about the resurrection of the dead (1 Thess. 4:16–17) and the final judgment (Rev. 20:11–13).

Whenever Christ returns, we know that we will all die some-day. We need to commit to a relationship with Jesus, however small our faith steps may be. Readiness means believing in him, following him, trusting his power, and trusting his merciful desire to save us regardless of all our sins and failures. As Noah heard and acted upon God's call, so can we in our own circumstances.

Prayer

Divine Savior, killed on a cross of wood: we go about our daily lives, and for many of us, you come in and out of our awareness, like a rainbow we notice, and then we move on. Cultivate in us a closer daily connection with you, so that if a crisis comes, you are already the One to whom we habitually cling. Amen.

Digging Deeper

What does it mean to be "ready" for Christ? What would it mean if we were unready? The two fellows going to Emmaus weren't exactly ready (they didn't understand Jesus' death and weren't expecting any miracles), and yet they had some kind of openness because they did eventually recognize him and believed. Would you call them ready? How is a season like Lent helpful for your own readiness?

Tuesday

Abraham and Isaac

Genesis 22:1–19; Romans 8:32

In the Jewish tradition, the story of Abraham's near-sacrifice of his son Isaac is called the *Akedah*, the Hebrew word for "binding." It's another difficult Bible story. As you read Genesis, you know that there is a years-long buildup to the birth of Isaac. At some point in Isaac's childhood or youth, God commands Abraham to sacrifice his son to God. The text also never reveals Abraham's thoughts and struggles about this, but the story provides a heartbreaking buildup as the two journey to Mount Moriah for the sacrifice, with Isaac wondering aloud where was the sacrificial lamb.

Once at the place, Abraham binds his son and is about to sacrifice him. We assume that Isaac's throat will be cut, as an animal's would be. But an angel stops Abraham as he takes up the knife and commends him for his faith. A ram is nearby, haplessly caught in a bush, and Abraham sacrifices the ram instead. God re-promises to Abraham that, because of his faith, his descendants will be a blessing and will be numerous.

The place was called *Adonai yireh* (sometimes rendered, *Jehovah-jireh*), "the Lord will provide," which translates into the Latin *Deus providebit*, which is the origin of our idea of "providence." Traditionally, the site was the place where Solomon later built the Temple in Jerusalem.

But why did God put Abraham and Isaac through this ordeal? An obvious answer is that God was testing Abraham's faith. God wanted Abraham to surrender to God without reservation, which he did. But perhaps Abraham was testing God, too; if Isaac was killed, God would invalidate his promises to Abraham, so as terrified as Abraham must've been, he may have had in mind to see how faithful God really is. Perhaps it was Isaac's faith that was also tested, since the text does not indicate that he put up any fight. (The text doesn't specify how old Isaac was.)

In Christianity, this story is not surprisingly connected to Jesus, who fulfills the story in multiple ways. If it was the site of Solomon's Temple, we can draw a line between Abraham, Solomon, and Jesus, who is himself the Temple. As Abraham was willing to give up his son to death (but was prevented), so God was willing to give up his son on our behalf (Rom. 8:32, as well as John 3:16). As Isaac survived his near-death and "rose" to live, so Jesus rose from physical death and now lives forever. As Isaac was apparently willing to go through with it, so Jesus also was obedient to God. But Jesus was also obedient like Abraham, trusting in God. Jesus is often called "the lamb of God," a reference to his humility but also to the fact that, like a lamb, he was killed as a sacrifice (Rev. 5:12). Artistically, Jesus has been depicted as a lamb.

Once again, we see how biblical images come together in Jesus: a faithful responder to God, and an obedient son, and also a trustful offering.

When we studied covenant a few days ago, we thought about God's demanding love. In today's story, we see God's fidelity to the covenant and the risk God takes to have a relationship with humans. We see the risk human beings take to respond to God's love. We probably will never be called upon to suffer physically or even to die for God. But it certainly has happened many times in history and still happens in some places. It is to God we respond, who has already shared his life with us and blesses us now and forever.

Prayer

God of Abraham, Isaac, and Jacob, you became human for our sakes to be bound to a cross. Continue to guide and direct us as we seek your will. It is hard for us to think of suffering on your behalf—and of suffering at all. Help us know that there is a "big picture" as you help us through the challenges and changes of our lives. Amen.

Digging Deeper

- What is the biggest risk you've ever taken as a Christian?
- Think about a time when you felt tested by God.

- Many Christians over the centuries have suffered and died as witnesses to the faith. Within just the last hundred years, we think of Dietrich Bonhoeffer, Dr. Martin Luther King Jr., Archbishop Oscar Romero, Father Jerzy Popiełuszko, members of Corrie ten Boom's family, and others. Of course, millions of Jews gave their lives in the twentieth century, just for being Jews. Consider studying more about the Holocaust and Christian witnesses in times of distress.

Wednesday

The Bridegroom

Isaiah 54:5–8; Ephesians 5:22–32

One of the most beautiful books in the Bible is the Song of Solomon. Though not directly cited in the New Testament, it has been a favorite Old Testament book among religious contemplatives like medieval monks, for whom the expressions of love and longing beautifully express, in a poetic and analogous way, a believer's longing for God and heaven.[1]

The book is love poetry between two people and explores their feelings of delight in love-making, sensuality, longing, anxiety, and return. The woman in the poems is a strong person in her own right, who knows her mind, her body, and her heart. She's by no means a subordinate to her beloved.

In its long, male-dominated story, the Bible has stories of strong and notable women: Hagar, Sarah, Tamar, Puah and Shiphrah, Miriam, Rahab, Jael, Deborah, Naomi and Ruth, Hannah, Abigail, Huldah, Vashti, Esther, Mary, Mary Magdalene, Priscilla, Lydia, Dorcas (Tabitha), and others. The Bible also reflects some of the culture of the times in its depiction of women's roles. Men like Jacob, David, and Solomon had multiple wives and concubines. Women could be publically shamed and abused, as in the book of Hosea (2:10–13) and Ezekiel (16:37–39). Adultery was a capital crime, because it offended the man's ownership of his wife's sexuality, but often only the woman was punished (John 7:53–8:11). One commentator writes, "In a patrilineal kinship, a large measure of a man's honor depended on a woman's sexual behavior. . . . Men had various strategies for keeping their women honorable, such as insisting that women remain veiled in public, segregating them, and restricting their behavior."[2]

The famous depiction of God as "jealous" is another example: jealousy is an objectionable trait and can lead to spousal abuse, but in the ancient Bible text, it was a term describing God's

101

relationship with his people, as in our Isaiah text. We see what we now would call sexism and double standards in other examples in both Testaments. Some of Paul's language about the church presenting itself as "pure and blameless" before the Lord comes from this old view of the woman's chastity as belonging to the husband (2 Cor. 11:2; Eph. 5:22–33). Today we think differently about issues of sexuality, marriage, gender, and women's place in society.

Taking all these issues into account and acknowledging that God is not equal like a partner or spouse, we still have a lovely biblical image of the mystical relationship between God and his people as one of marriage. In the Old Testament, the relationship is between God and his people Israel, as reflected in other Scriptures like Isaiah 54:5–8. Rabbis have long been interested in Song of Solomon as an allegory of the God-Israel relationship. We've been seeing how the New Testament writers show consistency between their experience of Jesus and the words and actions of God in the Old Testament, and in the New Testament the relationship is between Jesus and the church, with Christ the metaphorical bridegroom, as in our Ephesians passage. Jesus also uses this imagery in passages like Matthew 9:14–15. If you struggle with an image of God as a hard-to-please, easily offended "smiter," the image of God as lover and nurturer is an alternative.

In the covenant, the relationship with God is one of love, fidelity, and devotion; God makes a fierce commitment to the beloved's well-being, always willing to go the extra mile—the grudge-free love for which 1 Corinthians 13:1–7 is often invoked. Song of Solomon also has the theme of unfulfilled desire; one lover hides from another, increasing the feelings of love. Medieval monks understood this as a way God acts too; God may seem absent and yet calls for us, which in turn makes us long for God all the more.

Think of the person or people you love the most in the world, and that will give you a sense of God's feelings toward you and me. To quote Desmond Tutu: "There is nothing you can do that will make God love you less. There is nothing you can do to make

God love you more. God's love for you is infinite, perfect, and eternal."[3]

Prayer

Holy Love, our Love: bid us welcome to your heavenly banquet. We are uncertain, limited, and sometimes we have trouble feeling your love. But in this Lenten season, free our fearful hearts to a loving relationship with you. Renew in us your Spirit. Amen.

Digging Deeper
- Consider doing a study of Song of Solomon.
- Do you think about your sexuality as part of your spiritual identity too? How do you reflect upon your sexuality during an introspective time like Lent?
- Do you feel loved by God? Many of us have emotional struggles that make it difficult for us to believe we are worthy of love, or we fear rejection, or have had a bad experience with someone we loved, and so opening up to love is painful. Think about the emotion of love as expressed to and received by God. What have been your experiences of loving and being loved by God?

Thursday

Job
Job 19:25–27

The Catholic order, Sisters of Loretto, which founded several schools around the country (including Webster University, where my wife and I work), uses this short prayer written by the founder, Father Charles Nerinckx:

> O Suffering Jesus! O Sorrowful Mary!
> We give you glory, thanks, and praise.
> O bless our works and guide our ways.

The suffering of Jesus (and in Roman Catholic theology, his mother as well) are powerful sources of grace and blessing for those who call out in faith.

If you're like me, you also think of Job as a notable "sufferer" in the Bible. His experience of pain has been a powerful source of consolation and strength. Have you experienced undeserved pain that seemed to have no purpose or meaning? Have you felt "tested" in your faith because of the sense of absence of God as you suffered? My wife Beth's first husband, Jim, as he struggled with leukemia, turned to the book of Job for help. Job's questions and anguish resonate through time. His friends' well-intentioned but off-the-mark explanations do, too.

I want to zero in on these verses, where Job declares:

> For I know that my Redeemer lives,
>   and that at the last he will stand upon the earth;
> and after my skin has been thus destroyed,
>   then in my flesh I shall see God.
>
> (19:25–27)

The words remind me of a number in Handel's *Messiah*, as

well as the upbeat hymn, "I Know That My Redeemer Lives."
Job hopes for a vindicator to step up and take his side. He may
not have been thinking about an afterlife or resurrection, for
the Israelites of this time had no such fully developed con-
cept. By this point in his story, Job feels unjustly treated by
his friends, who were talking past him and not really listening.
Instead, Job wants a helper, perhaps a heavenly one, to speak
for him.[4]

I'm old enough to remember when you could redeem soda pop
bottles by taking them back to the store and getting a nickel per
bottle. Also, our local A&P supermarket gave stamps with pur-
chases and you could stick them in a booklet and redeem them for
a product. My parents got a toaster that way.

In the Bible, "redeem" (Hebrew *padah*, or *ga'al*) is used to refer
to kinds of transactions, as well as obligations, as when a slave was
to be redeemed (liberated) under certain conditions (Exod. 21:8;
Lev. 25:39–55) and when a family member was in distress (Num.
35:19; Deut. 19:6; Josh. 20:3). "Redemption" is the word for the
practice of using animals for sacrifices rather than punishing the
individual.[5]

Not surprisingly, God is described as redeemer (*go'el*), especially in several times in Isaiah 41–66. God steps in when his people are distressed. God is the redeemer of the helpless and needy,
as we considered in an earlier lesson.[6] But then Psalm 130:7–8
speaks of redemption from one's sins and iniquities, and the con-
cept takes on new meaning.

Naturally the idea of redemption is connected with Jesus (Luke
1:68; 2:38; Rom. 3:23–26; 8:22–23; Gal. 3:13; and others). Jesus
buys us back from the distress and curse of sin and death. Jesus
takes our side and steps in for us—all the way to his death and
resurrection.

At the conclusion of the book of Job, the Lord responded to
Job by recounting the wonders of creation. As many of us do
when we share our grief and struggles with other people, Job
gained assurance by getting perspective on his own pain. Christ
gives us assurance in our grief by being our redeemer, one who
was also distressed and now takes our side.

Prayer

Suffering Jesus, though distress can break us down, we are in a better position than even Job to understand the help and meaning you provide. Help us to be strong in trouble, help us find faithful friends to support us, and help us to look to you always. Amen.

Digging Deeper

- Think of times when you or a loved one were in the midst of terrible trouble. How did your faith and your church community help during those times? Who or what let you down?
- In your hymnal, read the verses of "I Know That My Redeemer Lives." Think about Jesus' characteristics depicted in that hymn.
- Consider studying the book of Job in a church group with a good study book.
- Do you like the movie *The Shawshank Redemption*? How does redemption function in that story? Who is redeemed, and how?

Friday

The Sign of Jonah

Jonah 1:1–4:11; Matthew 12:38–42

Jonah is another Bible story I learned in childhood. God wanted Jonah to go prophesy against the city of Nineveh. Jonah, however, fled and sought to cross the sea. A storm came. The sailors attribute the storm to divine origin and realize Jonah is the cause. He asks to be cast into the sea, which the sailors reluctantly do, and the storm calms. The sailors believe in Jonah's God and worship him.

As the Bible tells us, a large fish swallowed Jonah. Three days and nights later, Jonah is spit out and lands on shore. Now obedient, though not really humbled, he goes to Nineveh and prophesies against it. To his surprise, the citizenry believe Jonah and declare a fast. Even the king undertakes actions of repentance and shame. God spares the city.

Jonah is more successful than other prophets, whose hearers paid them little heed and even abused them. Yet Jonah resents the repentance of the city and takes shelter under a shady plant. God causes the plant to wither. Downcast, Jonah declares that he wants to die. God points out that Jonah had pitied the plant, so shouldn't God take pity on a city where (God points out) the citizenry are rather ignorant?

Poor, foolish Jonah! Because he points us to God's compassion, and because he is flawed and uncertain like so many of us, Jonah points us to Jesus. At one stage in his ministry, Jesus was asked to perform a miraculous sign. He responded that no sign would be given to this "evil and adulterous generation" other than the sign of Jonah (Matt.12:38–45; Luke 11:29–32). "For just as Jonah was three days and three nights in the belly of the sea monster, so for three days and three nights the Son of Man will be in the heart of the earth" (Matt.12:40).

In connection to this reference to his eventual burial, Jesus invoked the repentance of Nineveh (v. 41); as the Gentiles of Nineveh responded to Jonah's preaching, Gentiles will believe in the sign of Jonah—Jesus' resurrection—and will condemn Jesus' Jewish listeners for not believing. But Jesus stresses that the resurrection is an even greater sign of God's mercy than Jonah and Nineveh (v. 41). The Pharisees understand the reference as a promise of Jesus' resurrection, and they remember it later (Matt. 27:62–66).[7]

Jesus goes on to mention (confusingly perhaps) Solomon and the Queen of Sheba. In 1 Kings 10:1–13, that Gentile monarch visits Solomon and brings him expensive gifts. She asks Solomon difficult questions, but the famously wise Solomon is able to answer them. Impressed, she returns to her own land.

Jesus is challenging his Jewish listeners. Gentiles (the queen and the Ninevites) responded to the authority of Hebrews (Solomon and Jonah). In a like manner, Gentiles will recognize the authority of the Jew, Jesus. At the judgment, Gentiles will testify against those who didn't believe.

We must be careful not to take Jesus' words as an excuse to boast that we're beloved by God and that other people are condemned. That's what the Pharisees were doing, after all; and Jonah didn't care about the condemned city. They thought in terms of "us and them," "outside and inside." We can rejoice in God's blessings toward us, but we must not be smug that we are "in" while others are "out." Jesus is teaching about the vastness of God's love rather than any perceived limitations on God's love. God's love is more inclusive and merciful than our own preferences in people.[8]

We've seen this before among these lessons: Jesus breaks down boundaries between people. Jonah is another such story. We can't criticize God for loving someone whom we do not. Jesus overturned expectations in his own time and continues to do so.

Prayer

Dear Lord, we are slow to understand that we should not judge others. We want to be loved by you, which is good, but also to be favored by you above certain others, which is not good. Open our hearts as Jesus sought to open the hearts of the people he knew. Amen.

Digging Deeper

How do you picture the final resurrection? What questions do you have about it? (Do we go to heaven immediately when we die, or do we wait in some afterlife state until the final judgment?) Who would you want to see in heaven? Be honest: Who would you not want to see in heaven?

Saturday

The Good Shepherd

Psalm 23; Ezekiel 34; Matthew 9:36; John 10:11–18

I have always been grateful for my very first parish, three country churches on a circuit in Illinois. The folks inspired in me a commitment to church ministries that has continued through my church work and my freelance writing. At one of these churches, I met a shepherd, an animal scientist who specialized in that particular farm animal. I also knew farmers who raised sheep.

In Matthew's Gospel, we read, "When he saw the crowds, he had compassion for them, because they were harassed and helpless, like sheep without a shepherd" (Matt. 9:36). We are all familiar with the beautiful words of Psalm 23.

> The LORD is my shepherd, I shall not want.
> He makes me lie down in green pastures;
> he leads me beside still waters;
> he restores my soul.
> He leads me in right paths
> for his name's sake.
> Even though I walk through the darkest valley,
> I fear no evil;
> for you are with me;
> your rod and your staff—
> they comfort me.
> You prepare a table before me
> in the presence of my enemies;
> you anoint my head with oil;
> my cup overflows.
> Surely goodness and mercy shall follow me
> all the days of my life,
> and I shall dwell in the house of the LORD
> my whole life long."

Sheep need care and oversight. A college friend who worked his family farm told me that you cannot have only one sheep, because it becomes lonely and does poorly. In groups, however, sheep are prone to wander and get into trouble. But sheep do respond to a shepherd.

In his book *A Shepherd Looks at Psalm 23*, W. Phillip Keller writes that, as a young shepherd, he lost nine ewes overnight to a cougar. "From then on I slept with a .303 rifle and flashlight by my bed. At the least sounds of the flock being disturbed I would leap from bed and, calling my faithful collie, dash out into the night, rifle in hand, ready to protect my sheep."[9]

He continues,

> In the course of time I came to realize that nothing so quieted and reassured the sheep as to see me in the field. The presence of their master and owner and protector put them at ease as nothing else could do, and this applied day and night. . . .The behavior of sheep and human beings is similar in many ways. . . . Our mass mind . . . our fears and timidity, our stubbornness and stupidity, our perverse habits are all parallels of profound importance.[10]

If we ever wonder about God's care for us, we should think of shepherds. They do not turn their back on sheep just because sheep do stupid things and are prone to mess up their lives. Shepherds are devoted to the sheep's care. So much more is God devoted to our care.

The image of Christ as shepherd, with a lamb in his arm or over his shoulder, is a very ancient artistic representation of Christ, still popular for Christians for whom the image resonates. An elderly couple at that first parish of mine had a print of the nineteenth century artist Bernhard Plockhorst's painting *The Good Shepherd*, showing a barefoot Jesus holding a lamb and leading the sheep across a rocky path, the ewe looking trustfully up at the Lord. The twentieth century artist Warner Sallman, whose *Head of Christ* is widely reproduced, also created a popular painting, *The Lord Is My Shepherd*, showing Jesus leading sheep across a pastoral landscape.[11] Such renderings of Jesus have reminded Christians of the tender compassion of Jesus promised in John 10:11–18.

The Greek word translated "compassion" is *splagchnizomai* and is used in the Gospels several times to describe the feelings of Jesus (for instance, Luke 10:33). The word literally means, "to have the bowels yearning." The compassion that Jesus showed was no superficial thing, no "pose" assumed by a distant sovereign. He felt his love in his "guts." His protective love arose from his deepest being. It still does.

Prayer
For today's prayer, recite Psalm 23.

Digging Deeper
Although there are still people who raise and care for flocks of sheep, shepherds are not as common today as in biblical times. Can you think of any modern occupations that are analogous?

Sixth Sunday (Palm Sunday)
The King on a Donkey
Genesis 49:10–11; Zechariah 9:9–10; Matthew 21:1–9

In this Lenten study, we have paused each Sunday to reflect upon the previous week's lessons. But today, the action begins. It's the commencement of Holy Week, when Jesus goes to Jerusalem and accomplishes what is needed for our salvation (Matt. 21:1–9; Mark 11:1–10; Luke 19:28–38).

Do you have special Palm Sunday memories? When I was a little kid, I thought it was cool that we had palm leaves to wave. In southern Illinois, we had deciduous trees, spruce, and other varieties, but not a palm tree in sight. Like Easter eggs, the palm branches became a happy childhood memory of Holy Week.

Today's story has layers of meaning. As we all know, Jesus enters Jerusalem riding on a donkey, in fulfillment of Zechariah 9:9, "Lo, your king comes to you; triumphant and victorious is he, humble and riding on a donkey, on a colt, the foal of a donkey." A king or other military leader on horseback is an image of power and dignity. Equestrian statues of leaders are usually triumphant. In St. Louis, where I live, there is a famous statue of our city's namesake, King Louis IX of France, atop a noble horse. In Zechariah's prophecy, the king is victorious and can ride a more humble animal, symbolizing peace and well-being. Zechariah's passage is an example of the parallelism in Hebrew poetry: the addition of the detail "a colt, the foal of a donkey" adds dimension to the phrase "humble and riding on a donkey."

113

Matthew's Gospel seems to take this Hebrew rhetorical device literally and has Jesus requesting that his disciples borrow both a donkey and a colt.

The words of the crowds and the waving of the branches is a fulfillment of Psalm 118:26–27, a poem that connects the exodus with Israel's future hope. We'll look at that psalm on Wednesday, when we think about Jesus as the "chief cornerstone."

The passage from Zechariah has an additional layer of meaning. The prophet alludes to Genesis 49:10–11, where Jacob blesses his son Judah.

> The scepter shall not depart from Judah,
>   nor the ruler's staff from between his feet,
> until tribute comes to him;
>   and the obedience of the peoples is his.
> Binding his foal to the vine
>   and his donkey's colt to the choice vine,
> he washes his garments in wine
>   and his robe in the blood of grapes.

This Genesis passage is another traditional messianic prophecy. God's people linked their heritage to the twelve sons of Jacob, and Judah was David's tribe, too. Jesus' connection to Judah via David is something that the New Testament authors stress (Matt. 1:1–16; 9:27; 22:42; Luke 1:32; 3:23–38; Rom. 1:3; 2 Tim. 2:8; Rev. 5:5; 22:16). In Jacob's blessing, the authority of kingly rule will always remain among the descendants of Judah.

Like David himself, who was the youngest of the brothers (1 Sam. 16:1–13), Judah was a younger son who gained honor. The older sons Reuben and Simeon forfeited their inheritance to Judah (Gen. 49:3–10). In a society when "primogenitor" was important, God chose someone who is not what social norms would consider "first" or "best." Jesus is God's only Son, but he rejects the more showy aspects of kingship and humbles himself, taking the nature of a servant in obedience to God (Phil. 2:6–8).

That humility surely worked against Jesus in terms of his popularity. It's de rigueur to point out that Jesus had acclaim on

Sunday but was rejected by Thursday. We see this all the time in our contemporary politics: how quickly a candidate or an elected leader can plummet in the polls if the populace becomes displeased or impatient. It's not just the attitude of Jesus' contemporaries; it's human nature.

Jesus knew what was coming, even as he heard the cheers and saw the palms waving. He knew that rejection, suffering, and death awaited him just days later.

Prayer

Dear Lord, would we be excited about Jesus on Sunday and discouraged with him by Thursday? Likely we would, considering how our faith is strong or weak depending on the changes of our lives. Yet you love us faithfully, so please keep us steady, leaning on the constancy of your love. Amen.

Digging Deeper

Do you have special memories of Palm Sunday? What does your church do for this holiday? Remember the connection of Palm Sunday with Ash Wednesday: in many churches, the ashes from the previous year's palm branches are used to make the sign of the cross on worshipers' foreheads. What does this connection mean to you?

Monday

Jesus Cleanses the Temple

Psalm 69:9; Jeremiah 7:8–15; John 2:13–22

We have been seeing how different stories and words of Jesus can have multiple layers of meaning when we dig into the Old Testament. The incident in the Temple is another such story.

Jesus visited the Temple on different occasions during his life. On this, his final visit to Jerusalem, he "cleansed" the Temple. Significantly, the story is mentioned in all four Gospels (Matt. 21:12–17; Mark 11:15–19; Luke 19:45–48; John 2:13–19). John's account:

> The Passover of the Jews was near, and Jesus went up to Jerusalem. In the temple he found people selling cattle, sheep, and doves, and the money changers seated at their tables. Making a whip of cords, he drove all of them out of the temple, both the sheep and the cattle. He also poured out the coins of the money changers and overturned their tables. He told those who were selling the doves, "Take these things out of here! Stop making my Father's house a marketplace!" His disciples remembered that it was written, "Zeal for your house will consume me." (John 2:13–17)

I've heard people say, "Even Jesus got angry." As we saw earlier with Jesus' compassion toward the sick, Jesus put his whole, deep self into his relationships with people, even if (as in this case) his actions seem out of character.

This was not a formal cleansing of ritual impurity. The Temple grounds were huge, and thousands of Jews were visiting the Temple during that Passover season. Jesus' actions happened within a particular area and were likely noticed by relatively few people. According to Mark 11:18 and Luke 19:47, the chief priests and scribes did notice him, however.

What was the reason for Jesus' actions? In order for the thousands of pilgrims to have sacrifices, sellers provided doves that poor people would buy. Jesus objected to this practice, connecting it to the vanity of people with enough wealth to have more significant animals for sacrifice.

When he likened the trade to "a den of robbers," though, he was quoting a passage from Jeremiah 7:11. By quoting that Scripture, Jesus was making a powerful theological point less about the sellers than a whole attitude about worship. Many people of Jeremiah's time believed that the Temple was inviolate, and as long as people worshiped there, they would be safe from the foreign intervention understood as God's judgment against them.

Jeremiah warned that these expectations were wrong. (As we've learned, the Temple of Jeremiah's time was indeed destroyed in 586 BCE, during the prophet's lifetime). In that passage in chapter 7, Jeremiah likened the people of his time to robbers; they thought they could "hide" like fugitive thieves in the Temple from God's wrath against many, many years of faithlessness and covenant violations. Jesus, in turn, made a prediction of the destruction of the Temple of his time, which did happen, in 70 CE. He promised that the Temple would be raised up in just three days—but he was referring to the Temple of his body, not the building complex.

So here is another layer of meaning. While the Jerusalem Temple was an impermanent place of God's dwelling, Jesus' own body was a permanent "place" to which to go for God's presence. Of course, people of the time did not understand that, but after Jesus' resurrection, his words and actions became clear.

In John's Gospel, Jesus' actions were also linked to Psalm 69:9: "It is zeal for your house that has consumed me; the insults of those who insult you have fallen on me." This is a good example of a time when we understand Scripture more deeply when we see the context. Psalm 69 is also linked to Jesus' crucifixion, notably verse 21, "They gave me poison for food, and for my thirst they gave me vinegar to drink." John's use of the psalm points us to Jesus' suffering during this last week of his life.

Jesus was aggressive in the Temple in order to free us from ways that religion can make us hide, and he shows us we never have to do so.

Prayer

Dear Jesus, you are our place to go always. Sometimes we, too, hide our true selves by being respectable, churchgoing people. But when we take refuge in you, we cannot hide our sin, and you love and accept us as we are. Thank you so much. Amen.

Digging Deeper

Have there been times when you wanted to be more genuine with people about who you are, but you felt like you couldn't be? Have there been times when you felt like religion was a way to avoid harsh truths? During this Lenten season, what would make religion a potentially more open and openhearted experience for you?

Tuesday

The Day of the Lord

Daniel 9:26–27; Zephaniah 1:14–18; Mark 13:5–37

P art of Holy Week that we may forget is Jesus' "apocalyptic discourse" or "Olivet discourse" in the parallel accounts of Matthew 24:1–25:46, Mark 13:1–37, and Luke 21:5–38. Teaching his disciples during that last week, Jesus warns about the difficulties and persecutions faced by the Jews in general (as in the Roman war that would come in 67–73 CE) as well as the persecutions faced by those who believed in Jesus. Again, we encounter the theme of "readiness." Are we ready for whatever the future will bring?

In Mark 13:14, Jesus alludes to the "desolating sacrilege" of Daniel 9:26–27, referring to the Greek desecration of the Temple in 165 BCE as well as the future Roman destruction of the Temple in 70 CE. In Mark 13:24, Jesus refers to "the day of the Lord" of Zephaniah 1:14–18 and applies it to his own coming as the messianic Son of Man. In apocalyptic texts, "the day of the Lord" is the fearful time of judgment. The Scottish biblical scholar William Barclay notes several such texts: for instance, Isaiah 13:9; Joel 2:1–2; Amos 5:18–20; and our Zephaniah passage. The theme carries over in several New Testament passages referring to Jesus' second coming, like 1 Thessalonians 5:2 and 2 Peter 3:10.[1]

I've known a number of people who believe that these end-of-time Scriptures refer to current events. They also believe that Jesus will return in our lifetime. But many attempts have been made through history to predict the end times via biblical symbols: George Rapp, leader of the Harmonist sect, William Miller, founder of the Millerites, Charles Taze Russell and the Jehovah's Witnesses, and others. To me, the numerous failed efforts to connect Revelation to contemporary history advise against the effort. Jesus himself cautions that only God knows history's final timetable (see Matt. 24:36).

The book of Revelation is typical of the genre, showing the downfall of God's enemies. Jesus' own end-time teachings do caution about the punishments of the wicked, of those who are unready and otherwise estranged from God. While concerned about warning people, however, Jesus isn't interested in tabulating and predicting the end times in a fanatical, vengeful way. Jesus' teachings are less focused on divine vengeance of evildoers than upon God's salvation, as we saw in our study of Luke 4:16–30.

Recently I read a book that made an interesting point. The author noted how afraid he had once felt concerning Matthew 25:46 and its promise of eternal punishment. But the author realized that by the criteria of Matthew 25:46, Jesus' disciples were all condemned. They abandoned him in his most desperate time. But what happens? Jesus appears to them, loves them, and promises his eternal companionship (Matt. 28:20).[2]

Jesus warned about consequences to disbelief. He warned that people would call him "Lord" who would be excluded from the kingdom if they didn't do his will (Matt. 7:21–23). People could miss the kingdom of God and would be cast into outer darkness or into the fire (Matt. 24:45–51; 25:1–13, 30, 46). Yet even those who failed Jesus during his days on earth became overwhelmingly happy. People who discovered Jesus became filled with joy. Not only had they escaped God's wrath, but they had gained abundant, loving power from God in their lives that would carry them all the way through life and death to eternal life. They realized that Jesus suffered condemnation in their place. Jesus addressed the seriousness of sin with his love.

The evil and the suffering of this world will have an end. Jesus' words give us hope that God has the ultimate control over the world and the universe.

Prayer

O Lord, Alpha and Omega, we don't know the end times. We do know that eventually we will die, and we want to trust your mercy and power to carry us to your glory. Help us have the faith to know that you are faithful and powerful. Help us accept the reality of our eventual death. Amen.

Digging Deeper

Consider doing a Bible study on the book of Revelation. Are "end time teachings" an important aspect of your faith?

Wednesday

The Chief Cornerstone

Psalm 118:22; Mark 12:1–12; Acts 4:11–12

One of my best friends was married in a ceremony in a Roman Catholic church. Because of the contemporary design of the sanctuary, I noticed the crucifix more than I would have in an older and more Gothic interior.

If you knew nothing about Christianity, you'd likely think that a crucifix is a horrifying sculpture: a man who has been nailed to wood cruelly to make sure he didn't get loose until he was dead. But Christians believe that this experience of Jesus, now represented artistically, is a wonderful and holy thing, entirely appropriate for a room where happy events like weddings occur.

As Holy Week progressed, Jesus faced growing opposition. He was moving toward his execution. At one stage, he challenged listeners with the parable of the Wicked Tenants (Matt. 21:33–46; Mark 12:1–12; Luke 20:9–19), and he drew on a verse from Psalm 118: "The stone that the builders rejected has become the chief cornerstone" (v. 22). Later, Peter affirmed the risen Lord as the chief cornerstone and the power of our salvation (Acts 4:11–12).

Growing up, I had a fascination for cornerstones in local churches, and the names and dates on the facades of buildings in our hometown's business district. My hometown church, for instance, has a cornerstone that indicates the building was constructed in 1900.

If you were installing a cornerstone, you'd want an attractive stone with which to work. You'd want a stone that would look impressive and meaningful once installed. In fact, you'd generally want good materials for your entire building project.

For God, "appearances" aren't necessarily very important.

Jesus was intentionally humble as he rode into Jerusalem. He certainly wasn't impressive when he was dying on the cross.

David was not the obvious choice to become king of Israel. When Samuel sought God's direction for a new king of Israel, God did not select David's brothers, who were older and more impressive. God selected David, who, though handsome and hardworking, was nevertheless the youngest. God chose a humble couple, Mary and Joseph, who were not even married, to be parents of the Lord. God does not always choose the obvious person to accomplish God's plans.

Here again, we have a confluence of several biblical realities converging upon Jesus. A noted scholar on the Psalms points out that Psalm 118 is a Passover psalm. Thus, it's connected with the Lord's salvation and restoration at the exodus. As a psalm sung in the Second Temple, the psalm gave the people a sense of hope by looking to God's past wonders.[3]

The psalm also has several sections written in the first person (vv. 5–18; 28). Early Christians identified this "I" with Jesus and connected it with his entry into Jerusalem during Passover time (see Mark 11:9), and in turn, the joy of the Palm Sunday crowd echoes verse 26, thus connecting this Passover psalm with the hope for a Davidic king (Matt. 21:9; Mark 11:10; Luke 19:38; and John 12:33). All things together, Martin Luther called it "My own beloved psalm."[4]

For Christians, Christ is the cornerstone, and the whole foundation is the biblical history of God's salvation. We're able to see Christ in the Old Testament, and we're able to see the Old Testament in Christ. Throughout the Scriptures, God has shown us abundant examples of and teachings about the divine love and righteousness and rescues us and remakes us and never lets us go.

Prayer

Sacred Giver of Life, your ministry that began at the Jordan River culminates during this time in Jerusalem, David's cherished city. Help us know more deeply the power and blessing that opened up for each of us thanks to your foundational work. Help us be born anew as we consider your experiences. Amen.

Digging Deeper

- How do you handle rejection? Sometimes it depends upon the person, who may either shake it off easily or only with great effort. How are you growing in this area?
- Memorize Psalm 118:24: "This is the day that the LORD has made; let us rejoice and be glad in it."
- Do you have a favorite psalm? If you don't have a favorite, take some time in the upcoming future to think about psalms you particularly like. Eventually, choose a favorite for yourself.

Maundy Thursday

The Blood of the Covenant

Zechariah 9:11–17; Matthew 26:26–29

The New Testament authors demonstrate what Jesus told his friends going to Emmaus: it was necessary for the Messiah to suffer, die, and rise in glory.

The day before his death, Jesus gathered with his disciples for what we now call the Last Supper. It was likely a Passover meal. The very name Passover alludes to blood, the blood smeared on the Hebrew houses so that the angel of death would pass over them. Blood had the power of life for the rescued Israelites, and Jesus announces the significance of his own blood. All the Gospels depict the Last Supper. Here is Matthew's account:

> While they were eating, Jesus took a loaf of bread, and after blessing it he broke it, gave it to the disciples, and said, "Take, eat; this is my body." Then he took a cup, and after giving thanks he gave it to them, saying, "Drink from it, all of you; for this is my blood of the covenant, which is poured out for many for the forgiveness of sins. I tell you, I will never again drink of this fruit of the vine until that day when I drink it new with you in my Father's kingdom. (Matt. 26:26–29)

In Luke's account, Jesus adds the word "new": "This cup that is poured out for you is the new covenant in my blood" (22:20). Thus Luke connects Jesus' words and actions with the new covenant promised by God in Jeremiah 31:31, which we studied in the "Covenant" lesson (Tuesday of week 5). In Luke 22:20, Jesus' words and actions also connected to the "drink offering" of the Torah, an important part of sacrifices where wine was poured onto the altar fire (Exod. 29:38–41; Lev. 23:13, 18; Num. 15:1–10; Num. 28–29).

The Old Testament sacrifices were done because the people were in covenant with God. There are other layers of scriptural meaning. That phrase "blood of the covenant" first appears in Exodus 24. Moses builds an altar at the foot of the mountain and sets up twelve pillars corresponding to the twelve tribes. Young men from among the people sacrificed oxen to God, then,

> Moses took half of the blood and put it in basins, and half of the blood he dashed against the altar. Then he took the book of the covenant, and read it in the hearing of the people; and they said, "All that the LORD has spoken we will do, and we will be obedient." Moses took the blood and dashed it on the people, and said, "See the blood of the covenant that the LORD has made with you in accordance with all these words." (Exod. 24:6–8)

I've known people who dislike being splashed by water when their pastor flings water and says, "Remember your baptism." Imagine having animal blood splashed onto you. This is the nitty-gritty of God's promises.

Later in the Old Testament, the phrase appears again in Zechariah 9:11: "As for you also, because of the blood of my covenant with you, I will set your prisoners free from the waterless pit." That reference to freedom connects us with the themes of freedom and covenant in Isaiah 42:6–7 and 49:8–9, which in turn connects us with themes of God's redemption in that whole section of Isaiah.[5] Zechariah's use of the phrase "blood of the covenant" also connects us to the Exodus passage of God's covenant with Israel. In turn, Jesus connects us to Exodus 24 and Zechariah 9, but also to the new covenant of Jeremiah 31:31.[6]

The Exodus-covenant drama that we studied earlier continues: the epic of God's salvation is re-enacted and fulfilled, the life of Jesus is given for our salvation. We are welcomed into a new covenant, a new relationship with God.

Prayer

Life-giving Flesh and Blood, help us "feel" your blessings and grow in understanding whenever we take Communion. Renew in us the loving-kindness that witnesses to you better than our words ever can. Help us experience deeply the wonders of your love as you renew your covenant with us. Amen.

Digging Deeper

- If you aren't already, consider attending a Maundy Thursday service.
- The word "Maundy" has two possible derivations. One is that it comes from the Latin *mandatum*, meaning commandment, and refers to Jesus' command in John 13:34 to love one another as Jesus loves us, as displayed by Jesus' willingness to wash his friends' feet. The word also may come from an old English word meaning "to beg" and thus refers to the practice of providing for the poor as part of our devotion to God. Think about how these two derivations go together.

Good Friday

The Suffering Servant

Isaiah 52:13–53:12

There are many Scriptures associated with Jesus' suffering and death. The Suffering Servant passages from the prophet Isaiah are perhaps the key biblical passages concerning Jesus's redemptive suffering. As with Psalm 110, which we'll study on Easter, it's hard to imagine how Christianity could have begun without this image. Imagine Jesus walking with his Emmaus-bound friends—perhaps sitting at the side of the road for a time—and going into detail about this passage.

Isaiah contains four poems that scholars have called the "servant songs": Isaiah 42:1–4; 49:1–6; 50:4–9; and 52:13–53:12. The first two songs refer to an unnamed ruler and prophet of God who proclaims justice and promise, though through peaceful and even unassuming ways. The third song refers to the servant as one who is abused for his role, yet he does not return the violence done to him. The violence done to the servant is more graphic and stark in the fourth song; suffering abuse passively and silently, he is killed and buried.

Remarkably, in Isaiah's vision, this was God's will.

> [T]he Lord has laid on him
>   the iniquity of us all.
>   . . . .
>   stricken for the transgression of my people.
>   . . . .
>   Yet it was the will of the LORD to crush him with pain.
>   . . . .
>   [to] make his life an offering for sin
>   . . . .

The righteous one, my servant, shall make many righteous,
and he shall bear their iniquities.

. . . .

[H]e poured out himself to death,
and was numbered with the transgressors;
yet he bore the sin of many,
and made intercession for the transgressors.

(Isa. 53:6b, 8, 10–12)

Much suffering comes from the fact that we are mortal; some suffering is the result of evil. Some is what we informally call "karma": the cause and effect relationships of everyday life. Social injustices, war, natural disasters, and other factors also contribute to human suffering. Rabbinic writings called the Talmud, as well as other Jewish sources, have identified the suffering of Jews as a whole with Isaiah's servant; Jews have experienced persecution and injustice over the centuries from Gentile cultures, including predominantly Christian cultures.

For the New Testament writers, the Suffering Servant is identified with a particular Jew, Jesus, who shares in the pain of his people. The images in Isaiah 52:13–53:12 of the Suffering Servant fit so tellingly the circumstances of Jesus' suffering and death: his rejection, the irony of his being "lifted up" (elevated in the air to be crucified), his wounds and his abuse that left him marred and nearly unrecognizable. But also, the words of the prophet explained the reason for Jesus' suffering: his acceptance of the punishment for human iniquity, the power by which we are made whole, the intercessory power of his experience of suffering and death. "The Tree of true life was planted in the place of the skull," as one of my prayer books puts it,[7] and so we may all have life abundant and life eternal.

Prayer

O crucified King, you are the Lord of life, placed dead and cold into the earth. Thank you for being our Savior and Lord. Thank you for going through so much for people you never met—like us who live so long afterward, and those who will live after we are gone. Amen.

Digging Deeper

If you are able, attend a Good Friday "Tenebrae" service this evening. Afterward, write down your feelings about it.

Holy Saturday

Cursed on a Tree

Deuteronomy 21:22–23; Galatians 3:13–14

Friday afternoon, Jesus was taken down from the cross, a difficult task lest his limp and lifeless body fall to the ground. The "deposition" is a popular theme in art, with famous works by Michelangelo, Caravaggio, and others. Acting from the kindness and righteousness taught by their religion, Joseph of Arimathea and Nicodemus take care of the man's body, prepare it for burial, and place it in a tomb donated by Joseph (John 19:38–42).

These were lovely gestures of respect and compassion for a man who had endured so many indignities during his last hours. Even the casting of lots for his garments was so callous and awful: the guy is going to be dead soon, so let's just take his clothes. Yet Jesus is sufficiently important that guards are assigned to watch his tomb, lest someone steal his body and claim he rose from the dead. Grave robbery seemed more plausible than resurrection.

Jesus' body was on public display as he was crucified, but his dead body was not. It could have been: history provides examples of executed people whose heads or limbs were put on public display. You may be familiar with Sophocles' story of Antigone, whose brother Polynices was punished for his rebellion by being left unburied. Severed heads of executed people like William Wallace, Thomas More, and Thomas Cromwell were displayed on London Bridge. There was even a "keeper of heads" at the bridge. There are a few biblical examples of publicly displayed bodies as well (Num. 25:1–18; Josh. 10:26; 1 Sam. 31:1–13; 2 Sam. 21:7–14).

Our lesson today from Deuteronomy aimed at preserving human dignity for the executed by ordering a speedy burial. This also protected the land from defilement. The executed person has been condemned to a capital offence under God's law, and his condemnation brings a negative spiritual energy, so to speak, to the land, so he must be quickly and decently interred. Furthermore, people who handled dead bodies had to be purified from the resulting spiritual uncleanness (Lev. 21:1–4; Num. 5:1–4; 19:1–21; 31:19–20).

As an executed person, Jesus was "cursed [condemned] by God." And yet Jesus was God incarnate. "For our sake he made him to be sin who knew no sin, so that in him we might become the righteousness of God" (2 Cor. 5:21). God incarnate in Christ died a human death: God took on that impurity, that uncleanness. This, too, is a way that Christ embraced fully the tragedy of human nature—our fear of physical pain, our mortality, the horror of death—so that Christ's life sustains and redeems us, now and forever.

Jesus is in the grave today. He has "gone the way of all the earth," as his ancestor David said about himself (1 Kgs. 2:2). It is a Sabbath rest before Easter morning. His women followers wait for the end of Sabbath to anoint his body. The angels also wait. Jesus' male disciples are nowhere to be seen, but Roman soldiers stand by. Everything is somber. The miracle is just a few hours away.

Prayer

Dear Lord, new Tree of Life, we are concluding the somberness and sorrow of Holy Week. We are nearing the end of Lent. Continue to teach and guide us as we wait a few more hours for the celebration of your victory. Amen.

Digging Deeper

In some Christian churches, very little or nothing happens at all on this day: no services, no seasonal decorations, only emergency pastoral care. "Easter Eve," as it is sometimes called, has been called a Sabbath of rest for Christ in the grave. What are you doing today?

Easter Sunday
At the Right Hand of God
Psalm 110:1–4

Christ the Lord is risen today, Alleluia!
Earth and heaven in chorus say, Alleluia!
Raise your joys and triumphs high, Alleluia!
Sing, ye heavens, and earth reply, Alleluia!

Love's redeeming work is done, Alleluia!
Fought the fight, the battle won, Alleluia!
Death in vain forbids him rise, Alleluia!
Christ has opened paradise, Alleluia!

Lives again our glorious King, Alleluia!
Where, O death, is now thy sting? Alleluia!
Once he died our souls to save, Alleluia!
Where's thy victory, boasting grave? Alleluia!

Soar we now where Christ has led, Alleluia!
Following our exalted Head, Alleluia!
Made like him, like him we rise, Alleluia!
Ours the cross, the grave, the skies, Alleluia![8]

Charles Wesley's hymn has always been a favorite of mine for Easter morning. Christ has risen! In rising, he united his kingly and priestly aspects in a way no one dreamed. That is, his authority extends not only over social realities but also over death itself, over sin itself.

Since the work of biblical scholar Hermann Gunkel, ten psalms (2, 18, 20, 21, 45, 72, 101, 110, 132, 144) are commonly identified as the "royal psalms," written about the king and also the kingship of the Lord. Among these, Psalm 110 particularly caught the imagination of Jesus and his followers:

The LORD says to my lord,
  "Sit at my right hand
until I make your enemies your footstool."
. . . .
The LORD has sworn and will not change his mind,
  "You are a priest forever according to the order of
    Melchizedek."

(Ps. 110:1, 4)

Verse 1 is quoted or alluded to in several places in the New Testament (Matt. 22:44; 26:64; Mark 12:36; 14:62; 16:19; Luke 20:42; 22:69; Acts 2:25, 33–34; 5:31; 7:56; 8:34; Eph. 1:20; Col. 3:1; Heb. 1:3 and 1:13; 8:1; 10:12; 12:2; 1 Pet. 3:22; and Rev. 5:1). Whether or not we realize it, we quote the psalm in the Apostles' Creed and affirm the royal power of Jesus: "the third day he rose again from the dead; he ascended into heaven, and sitteth at the right hand of God the Father Almighty; from thence he shall come to judge the quick and the dead." As a fulfilled text, it gets a lot of workout!

In Psalm 110, the king is depicted poetically in a position of power: the power, in fact, of God. Thanks to the Lord, the king will rule with strength and righteousness. The last part of the psalm turns ugly and violent; through the king, the Lord will judge the nations (the enemies of God's people), shattering heads and strewing bodies. But such a promise was consoling during a time when God's people were beleaguered by hostile, neighboring kingdoms.

What is it about "the right hand of God"? I apologize that the following statements neglect left-handed people. Since a majority of people are right-handed, the phrase has come to refer to one's power and ability; for instance, Psalm 118:15–16, where God's right hand symbolizes God's strength and grace. "To sit at the right hand" is the place of favor. If you're left-handed, think of a favored person sitting at your left hand.

Who is Melchizedek? He was the righteous king of Salem in Genesis 14. Abram (Abraham) paid homage and gave the king his tithe. The king was also a priest of God Most High, and so he was a separate kind of priest of God (long before the Aaronic priesthood established during Moses' time). Jesus is understood to be a priest like Melchizedek, not of the tribe of Levi (where priests came from) but through the grace of God (Heb. 7:1–28).

Reading the New Testament, you get a sense of wonder and joy in the use of the image. After all, think of the way Jesus died. He died in a shameful way, designed to be a public example of how Rome handled troublesome people. To say that such a person now sits at the favored place with God, king and priest forever, is a bold statement.

But we are bold on Easter Sunday—bold and happy.

Prayer

Dearest, loving Lord, you conquered the power of sin and death by raising our Jesus Christ from the dead. He appeared to those who knew them and gave them hope and joy and power. He showed them how the Scriptures had foretold his suffering, death, and resurrection. On this Easter day, may the power of the Risen Lord open our hearts and minds to your love, open our hearts and minds into the meaning of the Scriptures, and give us faith and hope to follow him through all our days. Grant this through our Lord Jesus Christ, who lives and reigns with you and the Holy Spirit, one God, forever and ever. Amen.

Digging Deeper

Our Lenten journey is over, but our growth and understanding continue. Write down or think about ways that you feel you have grown during this time. What are ways you'd like to continue to grow?

After Easter

The Holy Spirit

Joel 2:28–32; John 14:15–31; Acts 2

Lent is over. Easter has happened. Jesus stays with his friends and followers for forty days, and he continues to teach them. He continues to teach us during this new season and beyond.

My family and I once had a Sunday school friend who wished aloud that she'd known Jesus in the flesh. She said she struggled in her faith (as we all do at one time or another), and to see Jesus physically would have helped her faith.

All of us learn from one another, and my friend's wish resonated with me. I realized that Jesus physically could not be in more than one place, and as a human being he could not be present forever. But thanks to the Holy Spirit, he can be with you and with me and with someone in a far away place, with no limitations. John tells us that Jesus assured his disciples:

> If you love me, you will keep my commandments. And I will ask the Father, and he will give you another Advocate, to be with you forever. This is the Spirit of truth, whom the world cannot receive, because it neither sees him nor knows him. You know him, because he abides with you, and he will be in you. . . . the Advocate, the Holy Spirit, whom the Father will send in my name, will teach you everything, and remind you of all that I have said to you. Peace I leave with you; my peace I give to you. I do not give to you as the world gives. Do not let your hearts be troubled, and do not let them be afraid." (John 14:15–17; 26–27)

Elsewhere, Jesus assured his disciples, "If you then, who are evil, know how to give good gifts to your children, how much more will the heavenly Father give the Holy Spirit to those who ask him!" (Luke 11:13)

If Jesus' first audience had been thinking about the Scriptures, they might have sat up and taken notice at the promise of the Holy Spirit. The Spirit in the Old Testament is a sign of God's power, for a particular purpose from God, as in Exodus 31:2–5; Judges 6:34; Micah 3:8; and Haggai 1:14. Of course, Jesus was conceived by the Spirit's power (Luke 1:26–30), so the presence and promise of the Spirit crosses the Gospel stories.

We also have this great promise from the prophet Joel.

> Then afterward
>   I will pour out my spirit on all flesh;
> your sons and your daughters shall prophesy,
>   your old men shall dream dreams,
>   and your young men shall see visions.
> Even on the male and female slaves,
>   in those days, I will pour out my spirit.
>   (Joel 2:28–29)

Joel's original intention is probably to convey that God's Spirit would be poured out to Judah, given the context.[9] Since Jesus' first audiences were Judeans, after all, they might have thought of Joel's promise and wondered if this was the time of this prophecy.

They were just a little early. Read Acts, chapter 2. The giving of the Holy Spirit was part of a process in God's plan. Jesus died, rose again, and then ascended into heaven. It was after this process of Jesus's power and glorification that the Holy Spirit descended to make Jesus available to all believers, for all time.

The Spirit was given to "all flesh," that is, all people. The trajectory of Acts is to show how the Spirit begins to be given to Jews and Gentiles alike. Remember our earlier lesson, when Jesus created a commotion when he announced that God's blessings would be for all (Luke 4:16–30). As we read in Acts, the Spirit begins to be given to despised people, like a Roman soldier, illustrating God's great mercy, God's breaking down of human boundaries.

And the Spirit comes to us today, in truth and power. Today, we may have lost the sense of amazement and joy of the first

Christians who received the Spirit. How do you know if you have the Spirit? Paul has a handy list in Galatians.

> By contrast, the fruit of the Spirit is love, joy, peace, patience, kindness, generosity, faithfulness, gentleness, and self-control. There is no law against such things. And those who belong to Christ Jesus have crucified the flesh with its passions and desires. If we live by the Spirit, let us also be guided by the Spirit. (Gal. 5:22–25)

Just as regular fruit grows, so does the fruit of the Spirit, showing how we are living by the Spirit's power.

Paul is even bold to say that we are "temples of the Holy Spirit" in that God's presence dwells within us (1 Cor. 6:9–10). As Jesus was understood to be the new temple (John 2:20–22), we too are places where the Spirit dwells. May we always be receptive of the Spirit's work!

Prayer

Holy Trinity, Holy Spirit, Spirit of Truth: continue to work in our hearts and our minds, in our thoughts and emotions, our good works and our good intentions. Give us power to sing your praise, to speak words of kindness and love, to express all our anxieties and concerns to the Lord. Support and mature us, for we are weak and prone to wander.

Digging Deeper

Read Galatians 5:22–25. How are you growing in the "fruit of the Spirit"?

Notes

Week 2: Jesus' Early Years

1. Tikva Frymer-Kensky, "Rachel: Bible," *Jewish Women: A Comprehensive Historical Encyclopedia*, 20 March 2009, Jewish Women's Archive, http://jwa .org/encyclopedia/article/rachel-bible.
2. Other ancient people besides the Israelites also had tent sanctuaries. The tabernacle, along with its furniture, is described in great detail in Exodus 26–27 and 35–38. Sacrifices were conducted at the tabernacle (Exod. 28:38–39; Num. 28:1–8, et al.).
3. Robert B. Coote, "The Book of Joshua," in *The New Interpreter's Bible*, vol. 2 (Nashville: Abingdon Press, 1998), 606–7.
4. M. Eugene Boring, "The Gospel of Matthew," in *The New Interpreter's Bible*, vol. 8 (Nashville: Abingdon Press, 1995), 166.

Week 3: Jesus' Ministry

1. Gene M. Tucker, "The Book of Isaiah 1–39," in *The New Interpreter's Bible*, vol. 6 (Nashville: Abingdon Press, 2001), 121.
2. Philip Barton Payne, "Parable," in Walter A. Elwell, ed., *Baker Theological Dictionary of the Bible* (Grand Rapids: Baker Books, 1996), 589.
3. Payne, "Parable," 589.
4. Talmud Shabbat 31a, quoted in Tracey R. Rich, "Love and Brotherhood," at Judaism 101, accessed November 21, 2014, http://www.jewfaq.org /brother.htm.
5. Tracey R. Rich, "Prophets and Prophecy," at Judaism 101, accessed November 21, 2014, http://www.jewfaq.org/prophet.htm.

Week 4: Jesus and Our Well-Being

1. Gale A. Yee, "The Book of Hosea," in *The New Interpreter's Bible*, vol. 7 (Nashville: Abingdon Press, 1996), 250.

2. Gail O'Day, "The Gospel of John," in *The New Interpreter's Bible*, vol. 9 (Nashville: Abingdon Press, 1995), 623.

3. Talmud Bava Bathra 9a, cited in Joseph Telushkin, *Biblical Literacy: The Most Important People, Events, and Ideas of the Hebrew Bible* (New York: William Morrow, 1997), 473–74.

4. Walter Brueggemann, *Journey to the Common Good* (Louisville, KY: Westminster John Knox Press, 2010), 39.

5. Ibid., 62–64.

6. Craig J. Slane, "Sabbath," in Walter A. Elwell, ed., *Baker Theological Dictionary of the Bible* (Grand Rapids: Baker Books, 1996), 697–99.

7. Huston Smith, *The World's Religions: Our Great Wisdom Traditions* (New York: HarperSanFrancisco, 1991), 321–22.

8. Ibid., 322–23.

9. Nils Alstrup Dahl, *Jesus in the Memory of the Early Church* (Minneapolis: Augsburg Publishing House, 1976), 120, 137.

Week 5: Great Themes of Salvation

1. R. E. Nixon, "The Exodus in the New Testament," section II.d., "St. Paul," [p.23]–[p. 24], accessed January 30, 2015, http://www.biblicalstudies.org.uk/pdf/exodus_nixon.pdf.

2. N. T. Wright, "The Letter to the Romans," in *The New Interpreter's Bible*, vol. 10 (Nashville: Abingdon Press, 2003), 508–14. He references Isaiah 11:11; 35:3–10; 51:9–11; 52:4–6; Jeremiah 16:14, 15; 23:7–8; Ezekiel 20:33, 38; Hosea 2:14–23 (p. 510).

3. Nixon, "The Exodus in the New Testament," Section II.j., "The Book of Revelation," [p. 29].

4. Gerard Van Groningen, "Covenant," in Walter A. Elwell, ed., *Baker Theological Dictionary of the Bible* (Grand Rapids: Baker Books, 1996), 124.

5. Ibid., 124.

6. Walter Brueggemann, "The Book of Exodus," in *The New Interpreter's Bible*, vol. 1 (Nashville: Abingdon Press, 1994), 951.

7. An excellent book that explains the Torah and its laws, which also brings in parallel Christian and Muslim beliefs, is W. Gunther Plaut, ed., *The Torah: A Modern Commentary*, rev. ed. (New York: Union for Reform Judaism, 2005).

8. Michelangelo and other artists have depicted Moses with small horns. Exodus 34:29–35 tells us that Moses' face shone with light. The Hebrew root *qrn* can be translated "horn" or "radiant light," and so the resulting mistranslation of the word set an artistic tradition of Moses with horns.

9. Brevard S. Childs, *Old Testament Theology in a Canonical Context* (Philadelphia: Fortress Press, 1985), 145, 150.

10. Theodore Hiebert, "The Book of Habakkuk," in *The New Interpreter's Bible*, vol. 7 (Nashville: Abingdon Press, 1996), 642.

Week 6: Jesus and Other Biblical Figures

1. "The [Song of Solomon] is a contemplative text. . . . It is not pastoral in nature; it does not teach morality, prescribe good works to perform or precepts to observe; nor even purvey exhortations to wisdom. But with its ardent language and its dialogue of praise, it was more attuned than any other book in Sacred Scripture to loving . . . contemplation . . . [intended] to foster a desire for the heavenly life." Jean Leclercq, *The Love of Learning and the Desire for God: A Study of Monastic Culture*, trans. Catharine Misrahi (New York: Fordham University Press, 1961), 85–86.

2. Gale A. Yee, "The Book of Hosea," in *The New Interpreter's Bible*, vol. 7 (Nashville: Abingdon Press, 1996), 208.

3. Quoted in Lorraine Kisly (ed.), *Ordinary Graces: Christian Teachings on the Interior Life* (New York: Bell Tower, 2000), 192.

4. Carol A. Newsom, "The Book of Job," in *The New Interpreter's Bible*, vol. 4 (Nashville: Abingdon Press, 1996), 478–79.

5. Dale Patrick, "Redeem, Redeemer," in Walter A. Elwell, ed., *Baker Theological Dictionary of the Bible* (Grand Rapids: Baker Books, 1996), 752–54.

6. Newsom, "The Book of Job," 478–79.

7. M. Eugene Boring, "The Gospel of Matthew," in *The New Interpreter's Bible*, vol. 8 (Nashville: Abingdon Press, 1995), 296.

8. Ibid., 297.

9. W. Phillip Keller, *A Shepherd Looks at Psalm 23* (Grand Rapids: Zondervan, 1997), 43.

10. Ibid., 44, 22.

11. "The Lord Is My Shepherd," The Warner Sallman Collection, Anderson University. Accessed January 27, 2015. http://www.warnersallman.com/collection/images/the-lord-is-my-shepard/.

Holy Week

1. William Barclay, *The Gospel of Luke. The Daily Study Bible Series*, rev. ed. (Philadelphia: Westminster Press, 1975), 257.

2. Matthew Linn, Sheila Fabricant Linn, and Dennis Linn, *Understanding Difficult Scriptures in a Healing Way* (Mahwah, NJ: Paulist Press, 2001), chap. 2.

3. J. Clinton McCann, "The Book of Psalms," in *The New Interpreter's Bible*, vol. 4 (Nashville: Abingdon Press, 1996), 1155–56.

4. Ibid., 1156.

5. Ben C. Ollenburger, "The Book of Zechariah," in *The New Interpreter's Bible*, vol. 7 (Nashville: Abingdon Press, 1996), 809–11.

6. Ibid., 809–11.
7. Mother Mary of the Orthodox Monastery of the Veil of the Mother of God, Bussy-en-Othe, France, and Archimandrite Kallistos Ware, trans., *The Festal Menaion* (South Canaan, PA: St. Tikhon's Seminary Press, 1998), 137.
8. *The United Methodist Hymnal* (Nashville: The United Methodist Publishing House, 1989), 302.
9. Elizabeth Achtemeier, "The Book of Joel," in *The New Interpreter's Bible*, vol. 7 (Nashville: Abingdon Press, 1996), 327.

CPSIA information can be obtained at www.ICGtesting.com
Printed in the USA
LVOW11s2358140116

470342LV00004B/45/P